Orijah

Urijah Meswaih

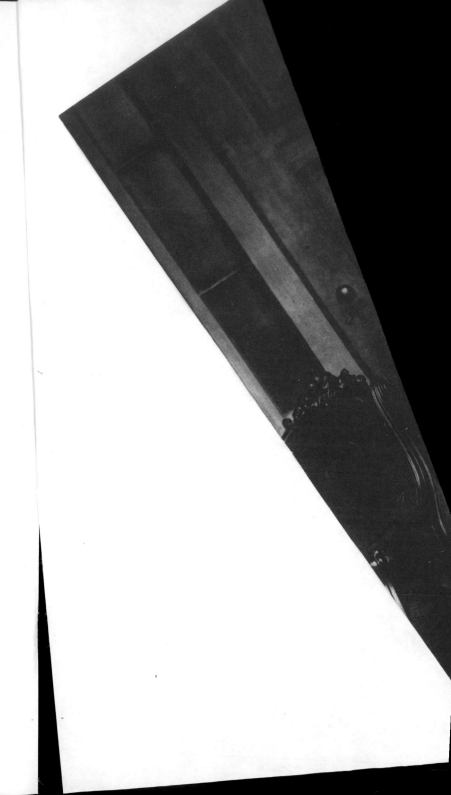

Robert
E.
Lee

Books by Manfred Weidhorn

Napoleon
Robert E. Lee

Robert E. Lee

by

Manfred Weidhorn

Atheneum 1988 New York

Robert E. Lee in 1865

For my parents, my wife, and my sons

Atheneum
Macmillan Publishing Company.
866 Third Avenue, New York, NY 10022
Collier Macmillan Canada, Inc.

Type set by Haddon Craftsmen, Allentown, Pennsylvania
Printed and bound by Fairfield Graphics, Fairfield, Pennsylvania
Designed by Mary Abern
First Edition

10 9 8 7 6 5 4 3 2 1

Library of Congress Cataloging-in-Publication Data

Weidhorn, Manfred, 1931–
Robert E. Lee.

Bibliography: p.
Includes index.
Summary: Traces the life, career, and achievements of the general who commanded
the Confederate Army during the Civil War.
1. Lee, Robert E. (Robert Edward), 1807–1870—Juvenile literature.
2. Generals—United States—Biography—Juvenile literature. 3. United States.
Army—Biography—Juvenile literature. 4. Confederate States of America.
Army—Biography—Juvenile literature. 5. United States—History—Civil War,
1861–1865—Campaigns—Juvenile literature. [1. Lee, Robert E. (Robert Edward),
1807–1870. 2. Generals. 3. Confederate States of
America. Army—Biography. 4. United States—History—Civil War,
1861–1865. I. Title. E467.1.L4W33 1988 973.7'3'0924 [92] 87-14500
ISBN 0-689-31340-3

J B
LEE

C 2

CONTENTS

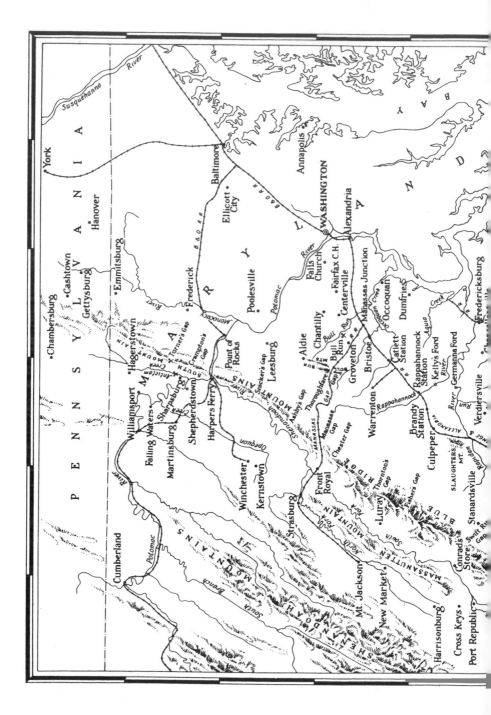

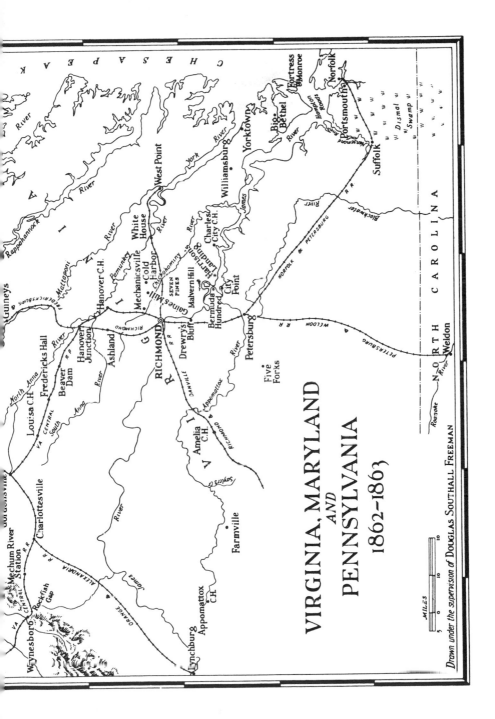

VIRGINIA, MARYLAND
AND
PENNSYLVANIA
1862–1863

MILES

Drawn under the supervision of Douglas Southall Freeman

Robert E. Lee

A photograph of President Abraham Lincoln taken in 1863, during the war.

1

A Fateful April

IN APRIL 1861 the new President of the United States of America, Abraham Lincoln, conferred with his closest advisers in a series of emergency meetings. Among the many burning issues under discussion was the importance of keeping a certain Colonel Robert Edward Lee of Virginia in the Army. Finally, Lincoln made—or approved—the decision to offer this man, who had only recently been promoted to Colonel, the awesome job of commanding a large new army. Then, as the meeting adjourned, the President walked to the window of his office and looked out at a Washington drenched in sunlit, blooming splendor.

April is the time of rebirth in nature and hope and love among human beings. But in 1861, the United States, not yet one hundred years old, seemed nearer death. What had begun as a noble rebellion against tyranny, a heroic fight against hopeless odds, and an experiment in a new kind of democratic government was on the verge of coming to a bitter end.

Blessed in its hearty people, its vast land, its bountiful resources, its freedoms, its splendid isolation from the corruptions of the Old World, the United States had nevertheless had a corruption of its own: slavery. In the Southern states, black people toiled against their will, while their white masters often lived the good life in large manors. For a long time, some people, including great men like George Washington and Thomas Jefferson, had guilty consciences about this evil in their midst. But they were content to let God and time bring about the solution.

Time passed, and no solution was in sight. Gradually, the slavery issue rose in the list of national priorities. Various compromises agreed to in the past were becoming unworkable, and new ones could no longer be hammered out. Extremists on both sides increasingly raised their voices and backed their voices with actions.

On the one hand, some die-hard Southerners glorified slavery, justified it with quotations from the Bible, and wanted to spread its blessings to the many territories being settled in the West and Southwest. On the other hand, Northern abolitionists came to see the slave-owners as satanic and slavery as a wickedness that had to be wiped out everywhere at once. Peaceful resolution was becoming impossible.

In fact, rebellion was in the air. The Abolitionists were encouraging the black slaves to rise against their masters, and the Southerners were openly discussing the idea of seceding from the Union. "Secession" was a nice name for rebellion. But the United States itself had been formed by a rebellion against an oppressive, remote, unsym-

An engraving of Lincoln's first inauguration in 1861.

pathetic central government. This violent solution came easily to the grandchildren of the makers of the American Revolution.

Newly elected President Lincoln barely had had time to take off his hat and coat in the White House before facing the prospect of presiding over only half a nation or, worse, no nation at all. Slavery took a back seat as an issue; the central concern was the preservation of the Union. If individual states could pick up their marbles and go home every time some debate did not go their way, then the Union was a farce. Yesterday the snag might have been trade policy, today it was slavery, tomorrow something else. For the Union to work, it had to be accepted by everyone.

The new President was receiving bulletins almost hourly about turmoil and dissolution. Slave states were seceding one after another. Suddenly, the bonds of trust that connected individuals and groups by tradition and shared experiences were being torn. In particular, the United States Army had overnight become a question. It contained many officers and units with a strong Southern background. Could they be relied on to follow orders from Washington—even if those orders forced them to aim their guns at fellow Southerners?

War is bad, but at least it unites a country against a common enemy who speaks a different language and acts differently. How much more terrible is civil war, which divides cities and families and makes the enemy hard to recognize because he speaks the same language and was your friend, relative, or playmate only yesterday.

Therefore, at the very beginning of his presidency, Lincoln had to make sure of the Army. In a situation in which reason and laws cease to dominate men's affairs, the only thing that works is force, and whoever has military power runs the show. If Lincoln had a strong army under his control, the rebellion might be quashed quickly or even prevented, and he could then turn to the delicate task of healing the wounds through talk, persuasion, compromise. But if he could not rely on the Army, talk was useless and the Union was finished. The new President had no other choice.

Thus it was that Lincoln made the offer to Robert E. Lee, who, he had been told, was the best soldier in America. Lee would be given command of a large army to be raised quickly for the purposes of, at the least, protecting Federal depots and property in the South, enforcing Federal laws, and, at the worst, bringing rebellious Southern forces to heel. That he came from a border state contaminated by slavery was all the better. It would send a signal to the South that one of her sons was high in the councils of power and that this area should not feel neglected. It could also be a warning to the South that if one of her sons, one of the best and most patriotic Southerners, saw that his duty lay with the Union, then the Southern rebels were the ones who were out of line. A powerful Federal army acting gently under the command of a Southerner would be like a well-meaning, respected teacher using a ruler on a stubborn or ignorant pupil's knuckles for his own good and not like a foreign despot coming to mutilate and conquer.

The problem for Lincoln and his advisers, though, was where Lee stood. He was one of those ideal soldiers who had not mingled in politics, or looked for financially advantageous positions, or been pushy about promotions or assignments. He had gone through the decades dutifully discharging whatever responsibilities the Army placed on him, and he had kept his feelings about current issues to himself.

So the offer was made to the Colonel during that fateful April of 1861. Lee rode home to Virginia, across the Potomac, past the budding leaves and blossoming flowers of spring, his mind churning and too preoccupied to enjoy the scenery. He went straight to his bedroom, ignoring his family. After pacing up and down all night, he finally wrote his reply. Of all the people in that distracted land during those painful days none agonized more than Robert E. Lee. He had no difficulty in making up his mind, but that did not make the pain any easier to bear. He went through torture not because of indecisiveness, but because of the price to be paid for his decision.

What Lee decided reflected the man and the life he had lived before that fateful spring day.

2

A Fine and Private Virginian

(1807–1859)

ROBERT E. LEE (actually he always signed his name as "R. E. Lee") came from two of the oldest and most prominent families in Virginia, the Lees and the Carters. Two Lees signed the Declaration of Independence. Robert's father, Henry Lee, after making his mark as a student at Princeton, served prominently as Chief of Cavalry in the American Revolution. A colleague of the Marquis de Lafayette and a friend and disciple of George Washington, Henry was known as "Light-Horse Harry" because of his dashing personality, great talent, and heroic deeds. He went on to become a politician, was three times governor of Virginia, and was even talked of by some as a successor to the President of the new republic, George Washington.

Unfortunately, he had too much dash to fulfill his potential. He was not very good at politics and peacetime activities. He could be moody and arrogant. And his later years were ruined by fruitless speculation in land and money.

After becoming a widower, Henry Lee remarried at the

Anne Hill Carter, Lee's mother, was born into one of the richest families in Virginia.

Robert E. Lee's father was "Light-Horse Harry" Lee, a hero of the American Revolution.

age of 37. His very young wife, Ann Hill Carter, was a child of the richest family in Virginia. Into this marriage, Robert Edward Lee was born on January 19, 1807.

The boy could not have had a happy childhood. By this time, his father's career was already falling apart. Owing money to many people who insisted on getting it back right away, Henry Lee had to sell his manor house when Robert was three years old and settle the family in a small place in town. The boy saw little of his father.

Then, Henry Lee came to the defense of an editor who was attacked by a mob supporting the War of 1812 against Britain. He was beaten and tortured. Broken in health, disfigured, depressed, he left without his family for the Caribbean islands and, a few years later, died on his way home. It was a strange and sad end to the life of "Light-Horse Harry," which had begun so brilliantly.

Now, Robert's mother was more than ever on her own, with five children to take care of. She was helped by her many relatives, of course, but life was not easy and her health was poor. Robert grew up an aristocrat beset by poverty.

Lee does not seem to have been attracted to any career other than the one in which his father had been at his best. Perhaps he looked upon military service as a family heritage or as something that tied him to a father he had little known. Perhaps he had no other great skills or interests. So he went to the United States Military Academy at West Point, in New York State, the college that has turned out some of the best and most famous officers in American history.

West Point in 1825 was a small school, and its students (or "cadets") were not always known for clean living. Lee was able to make friends easily, to participate in innocent fun, and at the same time to steer clear of the students' less admirable activities. He managed the difficult feat of being upright without being rigid.

Lee took his studies seriously and always ranked high. Graduating second in his class, he was the first cadet ever not to have a single demerit. Along the way, he also came to know many young men at the Academy with whom he would have important dealings decades later, whether as enemy general or as colleague.

After he graduated, Lee went home to care for his crippled and dying mother. Theirs was a strong emotional bond, as she had had to be both father and mother to him. If some mothers are accused of having unintentionally spoiled or ruined their sons with too much love, Mrs. Ann Lee was not one of them. Raising him more as a conservative, prudent Carter than as a brilliant, erratic Lee, she virtually single-handedly turned Robert into a man of integrity and decency.

In 1830, two years after the death of his mother, Lee married Mary Custis, a distant relative whom he had known all his life. Her father was the adopted son of George Washington. Thus, in addition to coming from two prominent families and having grown up with the spirit of the already legendary first President all about him in northern Virginia, Lee now found himself actually a part of the beloved Washington's family. He became the representative of the family of the Father of his Country, the closest thing democratic America had to a first family or an aristocracy.

The Lees soon started what was to be a large family: three sons (Custis, Rooney, Robert Jr.) and four daughters (Mary,

*Mary Randolph Custis, R. E. Lee's wife, was the
great-granddaughter of Martha Washington.*

Ann, Agnes, Mildred). Robert was a loving father to them,
at least during the times when military duties did not take
him away. He enjoyed playing with them and, particularly,
telling them long stories.

The early years of the growing family were marked by a
nomadic lifestyle and rootlessness typical of army families
burdened with periodically changing tours of duty. At West
Point, he had, like most of the best students there, chosen

Robert E. Lee in the dress uniform of a Lieutenant of Engineers, United States Army, 1838.

to specialize in the Engineering Corps of the Army. His first job as an officer was to oversee the building of a fort on a dreary island near Savannah, Georgia. Then, after an equally disagreeable tour of duty in an office job in the capital city of Washington, Lee was sent to St. Louis, Missouri, in 1837. His assignment was to redirect the flow of the Mississippi River to prevent the port from being destroyed by the current. This he did so successfully during the next two-and-a-half years that the city underwent a commercial boom as a result. He was promoted to the rank of Captain of Engineers and acquired something of a reputation as a rising star in the Army.

His next assignment took him to New York City, where he spent the years 1841 to 1846 working on the modernization of four fortresses that guarded the entrance to that very important harbor. His headquarters and his home were at Fort Hamilton, in what was then a suburb of New York known as Brooklyn. In 1844, he also served as an examiner at West Point during final examination week, and there he daily met with General Winfield Scott, the Commander in Chief of the Army.

So far, life in the Army had not been all that drastically different from life as a civilian engineer in a construction company. That was the disadvantage—or advantage—of being a soldier in a relatively peaceful country far away from the national rivalries of Europe. That peace was temporarily interrupted, however, by the Mexican–American War of 1846–1847.

As the people of the original thirteen colonies moved westward, they came into conflict with the Spanish-speaking settlers to the southwest. Tensions rose, especially in California, New Mexico, and Texas, where the boundaries were not always drawn precisely. After some armed clashes, war was declared with Mexico over the American annexation of Texas.

Lee was assigned to the army invading Mexico and performed some fine scouting (intelligence) work. In the following year, he was moved to the staff of General Winfield Scott himself. Scott decided to finish the conflict early by

General Winfield Scott, Commander in Chief of the United States Army. Lee served under him in the Mexican War, 1846–1847.

leading an overseas rather than overland expedition to Vera Cruz and, ultimately, to the capital city, Mexico City.

Lee participated in the planning of what was then considered a great enterprise. The operation went smoothly. It was, in fact, the first successful drawn-out military expedition in American history.

In the course of the campaign, Lee played important roles in the work of planning, engineering, and reconnaissance, as well as in battle. He surveyed the best route for the troops to take, especially in approaching Mexico City, and learned to work in the line of fire without losing his nerve. He supervised the movement and use of artillery. He directed bombardments and assault troops and participated in all of the three battles to take the Mexican capital. At one point he was on his horse for thirty-six consecutive hours. Conscientious and capable, he got along equally well with superiors, with colleagues, and with the men in the ranks.

As a result, he was promoted to Major, and, more than any other officer, was singled out by General Scott for special citation for intelligence and courage. Various generals took note of Lee's qualities and contributions, but he particularly impressed Scott, who called him the finest officer in the Army, "the very best soldier that I ever saw in the field." It was a reputation within the Army only; to the general public, he was known only because of his family and his wife's family, not his military deeds.

As important for the future as his advancement as a field officer was his experience at headquarters. As virtually the Army's top engineering officer, Lee took part in staff strategy sessions at the highest levels. He had a chance to see the workings of the military mind, whether in the discussions of the staff or in the way the Commander in Chief acted on information. In this, his only experience with full-scale war, he learned much about being a general, about carrying out military plans, about taking advantage of openings discovered in the course of information gathering—the daring gambles a general like Scott took and won. And, as at West

Point, he came to know many men who would play prominent roles in the Civil War.

Now it was back to peacetime routine and to engineering work on Atlantic coastal defenses, this time in Baltimore, Maryland. Then, to his surprise, he was picked in 1852 to be Superintendent (Principal) of West Point. Feeling that he lacked the qualifications and experience for such a prestigious job, he only reluctantly accepted it.

His old school, which his first son Custis was now attending, had grown in the intervening period. He served at this post for three years, and, during that time, tightened discipline and academic standards. He took great personal interest in the life of the cadets, and he established a good working relationship with his superior, the Secretary of War, Jefferson Davis. Though he did not revolutionize the Academy, he certainly improved it.

Lee had been a very good engineer and an outstanding soldier in combat; now he was a fine administrator. He had the requirements for such success: conscientiousness, intelligence, decency, and charm. He might have lacked the dash of his father, the genius of a Napoleon, the ambitions of a Caesar, but in his quiet way he made his mark in the Army as a reliable man.

Sometimes, of course, steady people, instead of being rewarded, get the worst assignments precisely because of their reliability. The men in charge, knowing that such men are bound by a strong sense of duty and honor that stifles complaint, simply take advantage of them. So it was that Lee found himself abruptly shifted from West Point to what the Army considered a more important task. In the wake of an Indian attack in 1855, Lee, a lieutenant colonel now, was made second in command of a new military unit in the Southwest. For the first time in his life, he had direct command of battle troops. But instead of fighting Indians, he spent much of the next five years making trips to remote places from his post in West Texas to participate in court-martials, that is, military trials of soldiers.

This was perhaps the most unpleasant assignment Lee had yet had. It took him far away to a hot and barely civilized country, away from his family and his home in Arlington, Virginia. He found himself having to travel long distances in order to attend boring trials, with their tedious presentation of evidence, reading of documents, and poring over small actions by small men.

Not only that, but the years had passed by invisibly, and Lee grew more aware that, despite all his work and his reputation for reliability, he had not been promoted as often as he might have expected. His salary had remained low, and he had always had a hard time making ends meet raising a large family. He observed somewhat enviously that some of his former classmates and colleagues had achieved higher rank or were making better money in private industry or commerce. They were not necessarily better officers and managers, but they might have been a little less gentlemanly in pushing themselves.

A certain melancholy hangs over these years, as if everything after the excitements of the Mexican War was an anticlimax. Such a downturn had happened also to "Light-Horse Harry" after the Revolution, but where the father had gone out in a flash of irresponsibility, the son was slowly sinking under the weight of responsibility and reliability.

Lee fared no better in his private life than in his professional life. His wife was disabled by a crippling illness. She required the same sort of attention that his mother had, and he, ever the dutiful, loving person, was there to give it. The death of his father-in-law left him with many debts and more responsibilities. He spent the winter of 1857–1858 on a leave of absence from the Army, working as a planter (farmer) on the Arlington, Virginia, home and plantation left him by his recently deceased father-in-law. Devoting himself to many pressing family duties, he actually toyed with the idea of leaving the Army for good.

The years 1858–1859 were especially depressing for him. Though there was talk of his being given high posts in the Army, nothing came of it. He saw himself approaching his middle fifties, noted the gray hair accumulating, and perhaps looked ahead to retirement, feeling himself played out, sensing that his life had been good and decent but nothing special.

The drift of the country toward civil war could not have helped his morale any. Yet it was to revolutionize his life. Instead of being unknown in old age, he was about to reach the high point of his life. The experiences stored up as an engineering officer in St. Louis, Brooklyn, and Baltimore, as a staff officer in Mexico, as an administrator at West Point, and as a good soldier carrying out innumerable other menial army tasks were soon going to be put to desperate use. Out of the national sorrow was to come his personal greatness and heroic achievement.

3

A National and
Personal Crisis

(1859–1861)

FEW AMERICANS of that period knew what was in store
for them, and Lee particularly had never involved himself
deeply in political questions. One incident that forced these
matters on his attention was the John Brown insurrection
in late 1859 at Harper's Ferry, Virginia.

Brown was a man seen by enemies as a sick fanatic and
by admirers as a savior of the slaves. Having taken to heart
the speeches of the Abolitionists, he urged the black slaves
to rebel and seize a Federal arsenal. The Federal government
declared him an outlaw and dispatched a small military detachment, with Lee in command, to put down the uprising.

Lee presented Brown with an ultimatum and demanded
unconditional surrender. When Brown asked for negotiations, Lee simply sent in the troops and ended the incident.
Brown was handed over to the civil authorities and
promptly hanged. Lee dismissed the incident as the work of

an isolated crank. He seemed not to have realized that it was a symptom of a drastic change in the way the national debate over slavery was being carried on. Reactions to the incident, rallying extremists on both sides, helped bring the nation to the verge of civil war.

Lee's unawareness was due not only to his concentrating on family and career rather than on public affairs, but also to the fact that he was no deep thinker. Though he had a fine education, he was not a bookish man. He lived by intuition, tradition, and feelings rather than ideas. He—like Washington, Jefferson, and other enlightened Southerners—condemned slavery and looked to the future to eradicate it. He thought that the institution was even more degrading to the white masters than to the black subjects.

As a Southerner, however, Lee had learned to live with slavery; he even had a few slaves of his own. He distrusted the Abolitionists for their fanaticism and apparent blindness, for their urgency and appeal to force. He was a soldier who hated violence, in word or action; the sight of a battlefield, he said, was "horrible." He therefore disliked extremists on all sides, men who would let their views on slavery imperil the Union. For his part, preserving the Union was more important than slavery, than "four million slaves."

Suddenly, the election of Lincoln and the prompt secession of states in the Deep South crystallized everything and made it impossible for Lee to avoid the subject any longer. He was torn now between love of country and love of region. He had based his life on a code, the code of honor of a gentleman, an American, a Southerner, a Virginian. And, at this crucial juncture, that code failed him. It could not tell him what to do; he was caught in an insoluble, tragic dilemma: Does "honor" dictate allegiance to country or to region? To the principle of federalism, for which his father had fought, or to the principle of states' rights? To the United States Army he had worked for all his life or to the values shared by all his relatives and most of his friends?

His allegiance to Virginia gave him an honorable way out. When the states of the Deep South had seceded, the border states were not sure whether to follow suit. Among these, Virginia was leaning towards secession, but her people, unhappy with that solution, looked for some way of healing the breach. The state sent a three-man committee to Washington, D.C., to try to patch things up. There was a chance that Virginia might opt for loyalty or neutrality. Lee's plan was to follow his state into neutrality. Resigning his army post, he would neither join the rebels against his country nor lead Union soldiers against his kinsmen. He would draw his sword only on behalf of Virginia.

This was not just a rationalization or a coward's way out. If he thought of himself as an American and a Southerner, he thought even more of himself as a Virginian. His allegiance, like that of many people at that time, went first to his state. Because the Union was still new, a person's feelings toward his state was almost like those of a citizen of one of the countries of Europe.

Virginia, moreover, gave him much to be proud of. The largest and most powerful state, it was the home of many of the Founding Fathers and Presidents—Washington, Jefferson, Madison, Monroe—who were the American version of an aristocracy. Geographically at the center of the United States, it was at the crossroads of North and South. It even lay, symbolically, just across the river from the capital of the nation. Lee could do worse, it would seem, than go with Virginia.

But no sooner had Lee hit upon an "honorable" way out of the dilemma than it was taken from him. Negotiations in Washington proved frustrating, and the Virginia committee returned feeling betrayed by Lincoln. Within a week after the first battle of the Civil War, the firing on Fort Sumter, on April 12, 1861, Virginia came down on the side of secession. The die was cast.

It was a terrible blow to Lee's patriotism: "I am one of those dull creatures that cannot see the good of secession." Yet he felt he had no choice but to follow his state into rebellion.

He might not have favored slavery; he might have been repelled by the fanaticism in the rebel camp; he might have seen through the foolish optimism rampant in the South among people who had little idea what a nightmare war is; he might have deeply regretted the demise of the once-proud United States; he might have hated having to turn his back on his career in the Army and on the many officers and men whom he had befriended. But he was a Virginian, and only devotion to God could be more important.

Unlike many of the Southerners he led, Lee fought on behalf of neither secession nor slavery, both of which he clearly disliked. He fought rather for the defense of his friends and relatives in Virginia against an invading army. As Jefferson Davis put it, "All we want is to be let alone." Honor, duty, dignity—call it what you will—dictated that a man must defend his state.

But if Lee placed his state above the States, why did he not place his God or his moral doubts about slavery above his state? Because most people in those days were not as outraged over slavery and racism as they have become since. Slavery was a traditional and accepted institution. Many a slave-owner regarded himself as a God-fearing Christian. Lee therefore saw nothing immoral in his decision. That he felt differently about slavery than did his neighbors gave him no right to impose his view on them, as the North proposed to do.

He also ignored, however, the possibility that they were on the wrong side of history.

Noble though Lee was, his personal code had confused or betrayed him. He had chosen Virginia, but Virginia had chosen racism, slavery, rebellion, and the past, instead of God, morality, progress, and the future. Lee is a classic example of a decent and honorable man who somehow ends up on the wrong side. America is greater and better as a result of his having been thoroughly defeated—even though he himself was, ironically, a much finer individual than most of the men who defeated him.

Lee's decision also involved a great personal sacrifice. Here suddenly out of the blue he had been offered by the Lincoln administration what must have been beyond his wildest dreams—command of 100,000 men (all units he had had dealings with before, even in the Mexican War, were only a few thousand strong), a chance to apply his Mexican experience in major battles against powerful foes, the trust and respect of the Federal government and even of President Lincoln himself. To obtain—after long years of toiling in obscurity, of being skipped over for promotion, of boring tasks and stifling peacetime routine, of resigning himself to genteel poverty, boredom, and melancholy old age—such a chance to reverse and redeem himself, a chance to make his mark in history at the head of a powerful army, to get what every officer dreams of (usually in vain), and *to have to turn it down!*

In that fateful April of 1861, Lee had a decision to make, an answer to give. As he paced up and down his room, with hands clasped behind his back and forehead furrowed, he went over the alternatives again and again. Always he reached the same conclusion.

The war was unnecessary; the cause was unjust ("I see no right in the matter"); wild men were in the saddle everywhere; he loved his country; the Army had been his one vocation, his home, his source of income, the recipient of the best years of his life and of all his abilities. But how could he take arms against "my relatives, my children, my home? . . . Though opposed to secession and deprecating war, I could take no part in an invasion of the Southern states." The big chance, when it had at long last come, had simply, sadly, too large a price attached to it.

On April 20, 1861, Colonel Robert Edward Lee resigned from the United States Army in which he had served for thirty-two years without a failure and in which he had participated with distinction in the best campaign of its history.

A moved General Winfield Scott said to him, "Lee, you have made the greatest mistake of your life; but I feared it would be so."

A mistake? Perhaps. Neither man could have known, though, what laurels Lee would garner in fighting nobly on behalf of a losing, and unworthy, cause.

Lee's wife said that, in arriving at his difficult decision, Lee "wept tears of blood."

4

Military Organizer
and Presidential Adviser

(*April 1861–May 1862*)

IN THIS PERIOD of national crisis, ex-Colonel Lee was seen as Virginia's man of the hour. On April 22, the state convention and the governor appointed him commander of all Virginia military forces—such as they were—with the rank of major general. He accepted the post with the provision that it be made clear that he had resigned from the United States Army two days before the new appointment was offered him. He did not want anyone to think that he had left the Army in order to better advance his own military career elsewhere.

The job Lee now tackled was to put together a Virginia army. Though it had long been looming, the crisis finally came with such fury and speed that the state was not on a war footing. With his administrative skills and experience, he was able to fulfill his assignment within two months. He created a staff and selected officers. He strengthened river defenses and arsenals. He put together and equipped a force of 40,000 men. He made provision for weapons manufacturing and for supply lines.

He also kept his eye on the larger strategic picture. Amid all the blind optimism in the South, he was not deluded. He declared, "The war may last ten years." And it would require much preparation. In the face of pressures for immediate offensives and even accusations of disloyalty, he urged all Southern commanders to keep to the defensive until a large Confederate Army could be organized.

The odds that Lee, and the South, faced were tremendous. The North had almost three times the population of the South (some 23 million as against 9 million, or, actually, only 5 million free white men). It had a far more developed industrial capacity for the manufacturing of war materiel. It had a huge superiority in weapons, in sea power, in large cities, in communications, and in modern efficiency. It had contacts with nations in Europe, while the South had a hard time in getting its ambassadors recognized by governments abroad. And it had the sympathy of the world. Though to Lincoln and the Federal government the main issue of the war was at first only the preservation of the Union, people in other countries cared less about the Union than about the existence of slavery and the need to eliminate that relic of barbarism from modern society.

Clearly, Lee had his work cut out for him. At first, he had troubles enough just in Virginia. Because it was the frontline state, troops from all over the Confederacy poured into it. The lines of authority became unclear, and Lee was caught up between state and Confederate orders. Finally, in May, the Virginia military forces became part of the Confederate

Army, and Lee entered the Confederate chain of command with the lesser rank of brigadier general. As commander of all Confederate forces stationed in Virginia, he was subordinate to other Confederate generals.

With typical modesty, he refused to make an issue of where he would be in the chain of command and of the fact that his new rank in the Confederate Army was lower than the one he had had in the Virginia forces. The important thing, to him, was to be able to contribute his talents to the joint cause in any way that his superiors thought necessary. And what they thought important just now was for him to oversee the transfer of Virginia forces into the Confederate Army and to prepare all the troops for battle. It was a desk job again. He would much rather have led the troops into combat.

Lee's family was no less deeply involved in the war. His two older sons enlisted and soon became officers in their own right. His youngest son and namesake, Robert, was a college student and eager to join up. Only with difficulty was Lee able to prevail on him to finish school first, as the war would be around for a long time. After a year, though, young Robert did join the army as a private. Lee could have easily obtained a special post for him but never considered doing so.

Even Lee's wife, who was crippled by arthritis, unintentionally became involved in the fighting. The advancing Northern army had early seized the Lee mansion at Arlington, and Mrs. Lee went to stay at the home of their son Rooney. Soon this home was captured as well. Rooney was away in the Confederate Army, but Mrs. Lee was caught in the home. Lee was greatly worried, but in those days opponents could be gentlemen. The Union General, McClellan, provided a special escort to take her to safe quarters on the Southern side. But then she was overrun by the Yankees a second time! Again McClellan gave her a special escort to safety—while, no doubt, exchanging a few jokes about her always ending up in the wrong place. She finally settled in Richmond for much of the war, and Lee every so often was able to visit her and their daughters.

In May, Richmond, the capital of Virginia, was made capital of the Confederacy, and Lee found himself dealing with Jefferson Davis, the President of the Confederate States of America. In these early days of the war, they got along well despite differences in personality and thinking. Davis was an intelligent man, but he had had lengthy army experience, and he wanted to have a hand in every military decision. He was also a person who quickly took offense, and his dictatorial ways irritated many.

Lee, on the other hand, was sure of his own abilities. His sanity and stability taught him to make allowances for the neuroses of other people. Besides, he had learned how to work with Davis years earlier when he had been Superintendent of West Point and Davis had been Secretary of War in the Federal government. Davis had then discovered what an able and patriotic man Lee was, and he loyally supported the Virginian in the face of much hostile criticism of inaction during 1861 and early 1862.

The criticism from the press and the politicians was merely one cross Lee had to bear. In fact, the first year of the Civil War was frustrating for him for many reasons. Eager to obtain command of troops and apply his military skills directly to the battlefield, he was saddled with one desk

job after another. He had to handle generals who were incompetent or actually only politicians in uniform. They spent as much of their energy fighting each other as fighting the enemy. He was forced to deal with politicians who thought that the war would soon be over and that drafting men into the army for a whole year was far too long—three months was enough! Instead of the current easygoing draft law, Lee wanted to see all white men between 18 and 45 drafted for the duration of the war, but he got only a watered-down version of this request.

In the first big battle of the war, at Manassas (or Bull Run), the Confederates won. Although other generals were seen as heroes of the victory, Lee, who was at his desk in Richmond during the fighting, deserves much of the credit. A quarter of the army there had been mobilized by him, and the strategy leading up to the battle had been mainly his. Still, while joining in the celebrations, he was saddened that he had been unable to take part in a major event in the "struggle for my home and neighbors." But President Davis, who had rushed to watch the battle in person, needed him for other matters.

One of the tasks the President now gave Lee was to do something about the western part of Virginia. The Confederate forces there were weak, scattered, and disorganized. The Union strategists saw a chance to open up a Western front in addition to their threats from the North and the East. So Lee went to the West in what was, in a way, his first service in the field for the Confederate Army and his first

Jefferson Davis, President of the Confederate States of America.

real command of combat troops. Officially, though, his job was to coordinate operations, not to be a field commander. He was still only the President's assistant for military affairs.

The resulting campaign was, frankly, a flop. It was marked by bad weather, rugged terrain, weak forces, poor morale, divided command, numerous blunders, and just plain bad luck. Lee had little authority over three supposed generals, actually three men with little military experience (two of them were ex-governors of Virginia) who just happened to be commanding military units and who thoroughly hated one another. No wonder Lee saw the task as hopeless.

Another difficulty he had there was a reluctance to assert his authority. One of the generals under his command was slow in advancing his troops, but Lee was too easygoing to order him to do so. This military weakness of Lee's sprang from a virtue that few people have—respect for the other person as a mature, independent individual. More a gentleman than an officer, he preferred to urge rather than command. Unfortunately, armies do not function well that way, especially in conditions of war. This fault was to plague him in the future. Sometimes a general cannot be a gentleman; Lee almost always was.

The campaign was a lost cause anyhow. The people among whom he had to fight did not see eye to eye with the more aristocratic Virginians to the East. Not approving of secession, they were an easy mark for spies and infiltrators from the North. Soon enough, the local politicians convened and seceded from the seceders. Forming a new state, West Virginia, they joined the Union.

So, after three months, Lee came back to Richmond in

October 1861 with very little to show for his efforts. The newspapers criticized him for being too cautious and inexperienced. He was called "Evacuation Lee," even "Granny Lee." But Davis continued to have faith in him.

One other thing he brought back from western Virginia was a beard. Rugged field conditions had made shaving difficult, and so he grew the white beard that has come to be associated with him. Unlike the beards and eyebrows of some other Civil War generals (Jackson, Bragg, Sherman), which made them look like wild, fierce warriors, Lee's gave him a kindly grandfatherly look that perfectly matched his personality, if not his fighting prowess.

After the debacle in western Virginia, President Davis made Lee commander of forces on the southeastern coast of the Confederacy. His mission was to safeguard the region from invasion or raids. The far superior Northern fleet was blockading the Southern ports by sinking stone-filled ships in the channels through which much sea traffic passed. The Yankees seemed to be preparing for an overseas invasion (as had been done in Mexico in 1846–1847) of the South Atlantic states. Stopping them seemed to Lee another hopeless task, even "worse than west Virginia."

He traveled through South Carolina, Georgia, and northern Florida on various inspection trips. His conclusion was that the two old, important cities of Charleston and Savannah, as well as the rail line connecting them, had to be the center of attention. Working with his customary great energy and drawing on his Engineering Corps experience in Georgia, St. Louis, and New York, Lee oversaw the strengthening of the defenses of the two main cities and forts. He brought the defense line further inland. He organized and equipped a force of 25,000 men. He concentrated his forces at key points halfway between the two cities so that each city could help the other in case of attack. He did such a good job that neither city, though heavily bombarded, was taken by way of the sea during the war. He thus brought security to the whole southeastern region of the Confederacy.

In March 1862, President Davis called Lee back to Richmond. The capital he returned to was different from the one he had left. The early enthusiasm for the war was gone. The South had suffered military defeats in Kentucky, Tennessee, North Carolina, and Mississippi. Ammunition supplies were dangerously low. Morale was poor everywhere. President Davis was becoming unpopular. There was a drift toward disaster. Politicians either daydreamed that the South had made its point and the war would be soon over, or fell prey to panicky fears about a Northern invasion and prepared to flee further south. Davis himself sensed the problem but was not dynamic enough to get a grip on things. Most upsetting was the behavior of General Joseph Johnston. The main Confederate Army, which he led, was supposed to threaten Washington; instead, it was being pulled back to Richmond. What frightened Johnston was the huge army of nearly 200,000 men armed to the teeth being put together carefully by Union General George McClellan, called by some "The Young Napoleon."

Lee was depressed by the lack of leadership, the unwillingness to face reality, the inability to take appropriate measures to cope with the rising tide of problems. By the same token, people did not pay much attention to a worrier like Lee. What, after all, had he done to make him such an expert? He had been a prominent army officer for almost a year of war without having fought a single battle. No one knew of his accomplishments, of the fact that his work of organizing was what gave the South even a chance of superiority over the North.

Naming him "commander . . . under the direction of the President," Davis gave Lee the job of coordinating all military operations of the Confederacy. It was another administrative desk job rather than a field command at a time of great peril, another—as he called it—"forlorn hope" assignment. He was only to be Davis's military adviser. Nevertheless, as usual, he got right down to work. Amid the mounting disorganization and despair, he discharged his duties excellently.

One of his greatest strokes at this point was to provide the manpower and encouragement that helped General Thomas "Stonewall" Jackson emerge as a military hero. Part of Lee's greatness was his ability to read character. Early in the war he had run across Jackson, who had done fine things at the Battle of Manassas. Like Lee, Jackson had the capacity to arouse the devotion of his soldiers, but he was in many ways the opposite of Lee. He was a strict disciplinarian, a grimly serious, righteous, religious man who demanded no more from his soldiers than he demanded from himself—nothing less than perfection. He even believed that there should be no prisoners of war; if he had his way, captured men would simply be executed. He had such strange ideas, habits, and tics that many people thought he was insane.

The serene and sane Lee, however, was able to see through the neuroses to the military heart of the man. Here

was one officer who was different from the average Southern generals. Most of them were more concerned with their
own external appearances, social lives, or professional ca-
reers than with the desperate struggles of their country.
Though he dressed sloppily, made bizarre gestures, and
sucked on lemons all the time, Jackson was one man who
had rare abilities, who placed country above self, and who
could concentrate his whole being on the military task assigned him.

Jackson was under the command of General Johnston,
but Lee quickly saw that for military intuition and daring
Johnston was not in Jackson's league. So Lee began to work
more and more with Jackson, going over the head or behind
the back of Jackson's superior to plan a campaign independent of Johnston's command.

Jackson had impressed Lee, and Lee had in turn impressed Davis. Thus it was that Davis took Lee's advice to
reinforce Jackson's unit. Jackson was to carry out a campaign that would distract the generals of the main Federal
army and worry the officials in Washington.

No less than three Union armies were approaching Richmond. Lee's plan was to have Jackson attack and destroy the
one in the Shenandoah Valley. This would force Lincoln to
pull the second army back for the defense of nearby Washington and relieve the pressure on the Confederate capital.
It was a brilliant idea of Lee's, and Jackson was just the man
with the brilliance to carry it out. In his almost incredible
Valley campaign of May 1862, he and his 16,000 men quickly
battered four Federal generals and 40,000 troops, piece by
piece. This was Lee's first bold stroke in the defense of
Richmond.

A new development soon overshadowed everything else: the behavior of General Johnston, commander of the main military force standing between Richmond and the North. Johnston was a proud, vain person. Jealous of other generals, especially Lee, he could not get along with President Davis either. He forwarded plans for offensives that both Davis and Lee thought impractical. When he found himself overruled, he resorted to secrecy and lying, acting on his own without consulting with the Richmond officials. Lee and Johnston had once been friends, and it was Lee's job to act as go-between for the President and the field general, two difficult men.

Now things rapidly came to a climax. As two Union armies were making steady progress toward Richmond, Johnston, with an army half the size of the enemy's, flitted about helplessly. He seemed to have too many plans, or the wrong plans, or possibly no plan at all. No one knew which was the case because he kept his ideas to himself. Lee urged Johnston to stand and fight as soon as possible. Johnston talked of abandoning Norfolk and other areas in order to make a stand uncomfortably close to the Confederate capital.

There took place a dramatic cabinet session in an atmosphere of crisis. Even President Davis indicated a growing readiness to consider abandoning Richmond itself. He asked Lee for follow-up plans. Lee had been listening quietly, and all eyes turned to him.

He spoke slowly, deliberately, forcefully: "Richmond must not be given up—it shall not be given up." Tears were running down his cheeks. The strength of his emotions and his military expertise shamed the others and stopped talk of sacrificing Richmond.

Persuading the cabinet was easy compared to persuading Johnston. A major battle was coming up near the Chickahominy River. Instead of making a stand before the river, which was the last natural barrier to Richmond, Johnston retreated across it and actually allowed the Federal forces to cross it as well. This was an irresponsible act. With the enemy so close, even a minor military setback would mean the fall of the Confederate capital.

Lee finally could not take any more desk-sitting in these critical hours, left in the dark about Johnston's plans. He rode out to the battlefield to see things for himself. Once there, he heard noises of distant musket fire, the sounds of a battle in progress. Yet Johnston insisted that it was only random artillery fire. Johnston was obviously close to being out of control—either he did not know what was going on or he was still withholding crucial information from men he was supposed to report to. Meanwhile, President Davis had independently arrived at the camp because he too sensed that something big was coming.

Soon enough the noises of combat grew louder, and the long lines of the wounded started filing back. The terrible truth began to dawn on everyone: A major battle was under way, and it was not going well. Johnston would have a lot to answer for. Unfortunately—or fortunately for him— Johnston was himself suddenly wounded seriously. None of his subordinate commanders could assume command because Johnston had not revealed his plans to anyone else. Things could hardly have gotten worse.

It was a grim, silent Davis and Lee who rode together back to the capital from the front, past the long lines of stragglers and wounded, past the moans, past the anxious-looking reserves coming up. Davis now turned to Lee and ordered him to take charge at once as Commander in Chief of Johnston's army.

After thirty-seven years as a soldier and after a year of frustrating administrative work, Lee was at long last given charge of a large army in the field during a major conflict. But if the command Lincoln had offered Lee in April 1861 had been morally and psychologically unacceptable, this one, a year later, seemed physically impossible to manage. It wasn't even certain, here at the very gates of Richmond, that there was an army left to organize, a country left to defend.

5

The Emergence of General Lee: The Battle of the Seven Days

(June–July 1862)

ON ASSUMING COMMAND of the "Army of the Peninsula" on June 1, 1862, Lee renamed it "The Army of Northern Virginia." It was to become one of the most famous names in military history. But just then, when Lee took over, few people could have suspected what was to come. His reputation was still unremarkable, and his appointment was greeted with criticism and ridicule. Could the man who had failed in western Virginia be even as good as Joe Johnston?

One of the first things Lee did was to give the army greater mobility by requiring the building of earthworks and trenches in front of Richmond. Such fortifications would enable a small force to defend the city and free most of the soldiers for offensive operations. The earthworks required lots of digging by soldiers and officers, many of whom were used to leaving hard manual labor to the slaves. Making daily visits to encourage the men, Lee had to coax them into rolling up their sleeves. The press complained that he believed more in digging than in fighting and derisively dubbed him the "King of Spades."

Lee got President Davis to reinforce his army with troops from the Atlantic coast and to strengthen Jackson's forces in the Valley. At this time also, Lee in effect invented the railroad gun. He had a large artillery piece surrounded with armor and placed on a train. A sort of movable fortress, it could be quickly transported to shell the foe from different vantage points.

Most important, he proceeded to impose a coherent structure on an army that, unlike the Northern one, was a collection of separate units. He saw that in an efficient military force, the soldier must identify not with the relatives who are in his outfit or with the place of origin his outfit represents, but with the army he is a part of. Lee's army became organized, centralized, unified—a large network directed by a single controlling intelligence. As one officer put it, "A new impulse was generated from general headquarters."

Lee's first challenge was, obviously, to relieve the Yankee pressure on Richmond. He decided the best way was to get away from the defensive plans that had been necessary while the South armed. Now, he felt, a quick surprise counterattack would disrupt McClellan's plans and "change the theater of the war." His goal was not just to push the enemy back home, but to destroy the main Northern force, McClellan's Army of the Potomac. And with his limited resources, he had to do all this without paying a high price in casualties and materiel.

Lee put together an ambitious plan. As he prepared for a coordinated attack, he brought Jackson back to the Richmond area for a conference. Calling his generals together on June 23, he outlined his strategy. Then he excused himself to go to his office to do some paperwork while his generals arranged the details among themselves. That was a way of operating he had learned from observing General Winfield Scott in the Mexican War: The commander takes care of the overall plan, and his subordinates apply it; the commander makes the strategy and brings his forces to the proper place at the proper time, while the generals of his corps and divisions handle the tactics. This approach proved a mixed blessing. When he dealt with men (like Jackson) on his own level of intelligence, the division of labor brought the best out of them. When he dealt with men not up to the mark, it backfired.

Lee's plan involved, among other things, a fake movement of Jackson's forces, together with the spread of rumors to make McClellan believe that Jackson was returning to the Shenandoah Valley to threaten the Washington area. Actually Jackson's forces were to join Lee's main army in a series of attacks on now one portion and then another of McClellan's widely scattered army.

At the same time, the dashing cavalry general, "Jeb" Stuart, was sent out with 1,200 men on an information-gathering raid. In an adventure typical of this colorful young man, Stuart circled the enemy camp and brought back valuable news about the position and size of the main Northern army. Lee's 85,000 soldiers faced over 100,000

Federals north of the Chickahominy River. Lee now left a mere 28,000 men to protect the Confederate capital; with the remaining 52,000, he crossed a stream and attacked a force twice as large in entrenched positions.

The first day of fighting, on June 26, in what has come to be known as The Battle of the Seven Days for Richmond, was a failure. McClellan had begun an offensive on his own, and only a quarter of the Southern army managed to fight. The great Stonewall Jackson had not moved into the combat according to plan. Lee's army lost a tenth of its men and had little to show for its effort.

The second battle went far better. The Northerners were driven away from the river. In fact, McClellan had to give up the attempt to capture Richmond. Here was Lee's first victory, though it cost some 8,000 casualties, a large number of them officers. In a follow-up battle on June 30, the Confederates won again, but, partly because of Jackson's erratic behavior, a great opportunity to surround and destroy McClellan's army was missed. In yet another battle, on July 1, the Federals managed to withstand the onslaught and to survive. Lee saw that more fighting at this time would be fruitless and called off any further attack. Instead he sent his recently invented railroad gun to harass the retreating enemy.

This fighting also involved members of Lee's family. After one harrowing day, Lee's youngest son, Robert, a private in Jackson's outfit, was napping under a caisson, when suddenly an army buddy awakened him because some very important officers wanted to see him. As young Robert staggered out of his sleep, rose, and tried to stand at attention, he discovered that it was his father and his staff. From

Lee and his generals. Lee assumed command of the Army of Northern Virginia in 1862.

his "father's loving eyes and smile," he gathered that Lee had come to see how his son was doing. Young Robert sensed that the onlookers must have thought it strange that

this "dirty, ragged, unkempt youth could have been the son of this grand-looking victorious commander."

Lee had other interesting encounters during that busy

week. After the first day of fighting, he ran into Jackson. Neither man looked like a famous general. Jackson was unkempt, and Lee looked so much like an ordinary soldier that one of Jackson's officers did not recognize him. "Ah, General," Lee said, "I am glad to see you. I had hoped to be with you before now." It was a gentle reference to Jackson's forces not arriving to battle on time.

Jackson muttered something inaudible, perhaps an apology.

"That fire is very heavy," Lee said. "Do you think your men can stand it?"

"They can stand almost anything. They can stand that."

Then a few days later Lee again met with Jackson, who was, as always, roughly dressed and covered with dust. Jackson talked in an intense way while drawing a diagram on the ground with the toe of his right boot. He drew two sides of a triangle and began to draw the third slowly, all the while talking on and looking periodically at Lee. When the third line met the first line, Jackson stamped his right foot with emphasis and said, "We've got him." Then he called for his horse, jumped awkwardly into the saddle, and rode off. Lee watched him for a minute and then rode away with his staff.

If "we've got him" referred to the destruction of McClellan's army, Jackson's statement was premature and ultimately wrong.

THE Battle of the Seven Days was Lee's initiation as a big-time field commander. On the plus side, Lee had stopped the Northern advance. The Federal army ready to sweep into Richmond had been sent back by a smaller force into a penned-up defensive posture miles away. Thousands of Yankees were prisoners of war. Many good, much-needed artillery pieces and hand weapons, as well as large amounts of supplies, had been seized by the Confederates.

On the minus side was the Confederate toll of 20,000 casualties. Federal losses were less by a fourth, and the South could ill afford such ratios for long. Worse, despite his great achievement, Lee was saddened that the Federal Army was not destroyed, as he thought it could easily have been. Besides an inferior artillery, he was saddled with just too many weaknesses in intelligence gathering and in the command structure. The enemy got away because, he snapped, "I cannot have my orders carried out."

Lee now saw that what had happened in western Virginia was no accident. In the army (as indeed in most things), having fine strategic ideas is not enough. One has to force less-than-brilliant people to take care of the details even while they do not understand the master plan. This means bruising the feelings of other generals. One battle in those early days was in fact jeopardized when General "Pete" Longstreet was "urged" by Lee to attack. Longstreet, with strategic views of his own, could not understand Lee's larger plan. Since he was not directly ordered to move, he did not bother to do so. Though Lee and Longstreet respected each other, they were to have other such costly misunderstandings. It is a definite stain on Lee's record that he either did not grasp the problem or did not do anything to remedy it.

Yet in the bloody Battle of the Seven Days, Lee had succeeded in changing the character of the war. The North had expected that a quick victory over secessionist factions by the use of overwhelming force would be followed by reunion. Lee's counteroffensive and victory had ruined all

that. Richmond was not about to fall. Reconciliation had
become impossible.

The United States had slid into a full-scale civil war. The
new goal of the North became conquest and domination,
even if it meant eventually resorting to total warfare, affect-
ing civilians, crops, towns. With its limited resources, the
South had a more modest goal: to keep up the fight, as best
it could, through cunning and strategic maneuvering, until
the Northern people tired of a war that did not serve their
immediate interests.

Another important result of the Seven Days was a marked
change in Lee's reputation. Until now, both sides in the war
had been finding their way in the dark. The generals were
in disarray, and the presidents were frustrated with them.
(Lincoln could not get McClellan to move fast enough,
while Davis and Johnston hated each other.) The advantage
the North had in sheer numbers, the South partly made up
for with enthusiasm and patriotic zeal. Now a great man, a
military genius, had suddenly entered on the world stage.
Lee was the first and perhaps only general to emerge during
the war with a mind of his own and a sense of the larger
strategic picture. His quick mastery of offensive strategy and
tactics went a long way in making up for all the disadvan-
tages the South faced. His rare combination of brilliance,
nobility, personal magnetism, courage, endurance, and re-
sourcefulness turned the main Southern army into a fear-
some fighting machine.

More importantly, Lee had shown a capacity for aggressiveness and risk taking. These qualities are essential if a
general is to be victorious, especially a general who has all
the statistics working against him. These qualities had been

missing so far in the Southern camp (and would remain absent in the Northern one). But Lee had daring battle plans, and he had taken, at long last, battlefield command.

Not only did he have the larger military vision, but also he could inspire men to fight to the death and against hopeless odds. The soldiers felt that he was the noblest and smartest of generals. He had their welfare at heart, and they could trust his intelligence not to send them out on foolish or useless missions.

In Lee, the Confederate soldiers had a general who could cope with any problem, but also one who clearly cared for them. He therefore quickly became respected, revered, loved. He and his army had become one thing, and one without the other was unimaginable. The Army of Northern Virginia is legendary not just because of Lee's mind but also because of his heart.

Even the meanest soldier somehow felt that Lee was his personal friend. Any man with a problem could approach him. He was a father to the entire army, and together they went through much joy and much suffering. After the initial enthusiasm for the war died down, the charisma (personal magnetism) of this man enabled the Army of Northern Virginia to overcome difficulties that would have destroyed any other army or general.

Lee was a fairly tall (six feet), broad-shouldered man in his middle fifties, with thoughtful eyes and that grandfatherly beard. He stood erect and walked with a graceful, dignified step. He was soldierly in his bearing, gentlemanly in his face, courteous in his manner. Usually dressed simply but neatly, he looked smart and clean even after arduous marches in heat and dust. He seemed to his soldiers and officers, as one of them put it, "the grandest specimen of mankind. . . . He looked as though he ought to have been and was the monarch of the world."

He also had a serenity, an air of confidence that was contagious. It gained him the support of the President, the loyalty of his officers, and the trust of his soldiers. He thus kept up the hopes and fighting spirit of the South through the darkening years. The men were now fighting as much for "Marse Robert," "Uncle Robert," as for slavery, secession, or their home state. And the most amazing part of Lee's greatness is that he, like few in history, remained unspoiled by his new-found success and fame, perhaps because his piety attributed everything to God.

Even in victory, he remained a man without personal ambition and without the arrogance of most officers. He had no special food reserved for himself. Like a common soldier, he slept in an unpretentious tent and with a single blanket. He would not allow his men to confiscate personal property. He refused to take over someone's private home or farm for his headquarters; his own tent was good enough. And in that tent there was no ceremony or pomp.

He rarely scolded people, and when he did, he was quick to apologize. He did not blame others for fiascoes. He did not browbeat or insult. An unpretentious, sincere, simple, gently humorous, charming man, he made great company. Lee was one of those rare persons who, as one of his numerous admirers put it, are "greater when near them than when at a distance," and "the more one saw of him the more one loved him." No man had more friends and fewer enemies. He never spoke with bitterness, even of the Northerners. His one major weakness—slowness to assert his authority—

came from that sweetness of personality that made him so loved and revered.

Lee also was incorruptible. It was common then for generals (as it is for politicians in all periods) to practice nepotism—placing relatives and friends in positions of authority for which they are not qualified. When Mrs. Lee urged him to add one of his sons to his staff, he answered that such an act, while it would be "a great pleasure and comfort to me, and . . . extremely useful," was "wrong in principle." He therefore opposed it. In any case, it would be better for the son to "rise by his own merit in an independent position." At another time, when President Davis himself wanted one of Lee's other sons to be made commander of a force, Lee refused to do so because the son was not experienced enough for the job. To bypass qualified officers for the sake of an unqualified man was impossible, "especially when that man is my own son." He would not ask any favor for his son that he could not ask for the humblest soldier in the army.

By every standard, the South should have gone under easily in a military showdown. And indeed, in the first stages, it seemed to be sinking fast despite some early victories. That it did not fall for a long time can be attributed mainly to the advent of one man. On taking over Johnston's demoralized and disorganized clusters of soldiers, he— "Evacuation Lee," "Granny Lee," "The King of Spades"— made this army his own, conceived and applied a master plan, and, by shifting the danger from Richmond to Washington, altered the balance of the war.

Lee himself may have been unhappy over what he had failed to achieve during the Battle of the Seven Days, but the rest of the South knew only what he *had* done and that was plenty for one week. He had removed the pressure from the heart of the Confederacy, revived the enthusiasm of Southerners, changed the character of the war from a defensive—a confused defensive—to an offensive one. The South had a new lease on life. And a hero.

6

Going North: Second Manassas and Antietam

(July–September 1862)

DURING JULY 1862, Lee reorganized, resupplied, and reinforced his army. He had to work fast because the North was cooking up more trouble for him. In August, Lee found himself facing a new Federal force coming down from the West, the Army of Virginia, headed by General John Pope. This man threatened to bring the war to the South's civilian population. Besides being ruthless, Pope was a boaster and, to boot, militarily stupid. No wonder that Lee disliked him as he did no other enemy general.

If Pope's 43,000 succeeded in reaching McClellan's 90,000, the 65,000 Confederates would be in dire straits. Lee therefore assigned Stonewall Jackson the task of harassing Pope's supply lines. This move represented a large double risk. For one thing, it violated a cardinal rule of military strategy: Never divide your army in the face of a superior foe. For another, the great Jackson had suddenly become a question mark. He had not fought well in the Seven Days. Indeed, he had several times let Lee down. But Lee was perceptive and forgiving enough to retain faith in the brilliant eccentric.

And he was right. Jackson was back in fine form, defeating a part of Pope's army on August 9. Then Jackson's 20,000 men went on an end run, over mountain passes and rivers, for an attack on the rear of Pope's forces. After covering fifty miles in two days, Jackson seized and destroyed on August 26–27 the Federal supply depot at Manassas Junction and disappeared. Pope's far larger army looked in vain for Jackson's.

Jackson had in fact rejoined Lee, and together they fell on a mystified, confused Pope. In this second and far larger battle of Manassas (or Bull Run), Lee's forces won their biggest victory yet and sent Pope reeling back in the direction of Washington. Every aspect of the military operation had improved—staff work, artillery, cavalry, intelligence, strategy, tactics. The Confederates had 9,000 casualties out of 49,000 to the Federals' 16,000 out of 76,000. Large amounts of Northern supplies fell into Southern hands.

As Lee rode through the camp, a young man covered with soot and grime from the battle waved at him. Lee stopped and said, "Well, my man, what can I do for you?"

"Why, General, don't you know me?"

Lee then recognized his son Robert. He was amused at his appearance and glad to know that he was safe.

Second Manassas is considered one of Lee's masterpieces. And, no less important, Jackson was at his best again. From then on, Lee and Jackson operated closely together, forming one of the great duos in military history. Both wanted offensive action and considered invading the North. Both believed in imaginative, bold ideas rather than routine military operations. Both were courageous, resolute risk-takers. Jackson alone of Lee's generals could, first, understand Lee's mind and the boldness of his imagination, and, second, carry out the plans in detail, and, third, be cool when things looked bad, as, given the disparity in numbers and the great risks taken, they were bound to. Lee therefore gladly granted to this kindred soul a semi-independent status.

President Davis gave much of the credit for the victory to Lee. In four months, the South, which was defeated or surrounded before Richmond, in the Shenandoah Valley, in western Virginia, and in North Carolina, had under Lee turned the situation around. Virginia had been freed, and Lee's army seemed, after a half dozen battles, untouchable. Instead of being five miles in front of Richmond, Lee's army was within twenty miles of Washington. Now it was the Federal capital's turn to panic and to talk of moving men and government offices north to New York. While the South might be outclassed in strength of arms, it was superior in zeal, confidence, determination, unity of command—the invisible things of the spirit that often matter more than material advantages.

Lee's imagination expanded now with his successes. At the beginning of the war, strategy had been dictated by politics. Since the South only wanted to go its own way, its military strategy was defensive, and the North had to take the offensive.

But Lee knew that the best defense is a good offense. If he carried the war into the North, the Yankees would think twice about imposing their will on the South. The war would go on only if the people in the North and their representatives in government wanted it to, and that depended on how well the generals did. They were doing very poorly just now, and the North was tiring of battle. Even Europe was drifting toward official recognition of the Confederacy as a separate nation. A sign of the North's distress was that Lincoln (as Lee did not yet know) was preparing the Emancipation Proclamation. The freeing of the slaves was meant to raise a new moral issue to bring support for the Union from those in the North and in Europe who had not responded to the purely political issue of preserving the Union.

Lee sensed that the time was ripe for weaning the Yankees from the war altogether if he could make them hurt at home, on Union soil. The goal was not conquest, as it was for the North, but just peace on the basis of Southern independence.

Naturally, the time to strike was while McClellan's army was still demoralized by defeat. The Army of Northern Virginia would cross the Potomac River and enter Maryland. This invasion would force the North to remove all its troops from Virginia for the sake of the defense of Washington. Maryland was a good point of entry because of the widely held view that there were strong secessionist feelings there and that only the presence of Northern soldiers kept it in the Union. From Maryland it is a short route to Philadelphia, Baltimore, or Washington.

That some 150,000 Northern troops were there did not faze Lee. For one thing, he knew that they were led by the overly cautious, nervous McClellan. Besides, he of necessity never calculated by mere troop numbers. If he had, he might as well have given up the war at the start. Such a daring plan required him to pry troops away from a President Davis worried over the vulnerability of Richmond, but at this time he and Davis still had confidence in one another.

So on September 4, 1862, the Army of Northern Virginia invaded Maryland. It was the first time Confederate soldiers were on Union soil. With typical daring, Lee divided his army in enemy territory and sent Jackson to seize Harper's Ferry. Lee issued a proclamation to the people of Maryland in which he asserted that the Confederacy looked on their state as one of its own. He urged Marylanders to exercise, for the first time, a free choice as to whether they should join the Confederacy. He promised to abide by the outcome, whatever it might be.

At the same time, in private, Lee urged Davis to make a peace offer to the North, a peace based on Northern recognition of the Confederacy. He wisely understood that such an offer, if made by Davis while the South was losing, would be seen as a disguised plea of "Stop, I give up!" and would merely encourage Northern aggressiveness and demands of unconditional surrender. But coming now, when the North was tottering and the South on the march, such an offer by Davis would have to be seen as a sincere expression of a desire for an honorable peace because it came from a position of strength, not weakness. However, Davis did not make the offer, and, if he had, the North would have turned it down.

In any case, the South's good fortune did not last long. The military operations in Maryland did not go as planned. The Marylanders gave Lee's forces a mixed reception, and the Southern army was plagued, as it was throughout the war, with straggling and supply problems. Shoes and blankets, especially, were sorely needed. Morale was another unforeseen difficulty. Some of the soldiers, coming from sections where slavery was not all that important, fought only to defend their homeland, not to invade the North. They—perhaps as many as 10,000—now left. Those who remained, while being enthusiastic and warlike, were dirty, ragged, and hungry.

Worst of all, there now took place one of those freak accidents by which very small things have very large consequences. Lee wrote out the complete battle plan and troop dispositions in his Special Order 191. When his generals Jackson and D. H. Hill had to go on separate missions, Jackson made a copy of the order and sent it to Hill. Since Hill had already been given a copy, one of his officers used the order sheet to wrap up three cigars. This was unpardonable recklessness with a document so important that General Longstreet, when he finished reading copy, shredded it with his teeth. As the Confederate units moved on, the package of cigars happened to fall unnoticed on the campsite ground. And there it lay.

Soon the Federal army took possession of the campsite. A private from Indiana, noticing the package, picked it up and opened it. He was delighted with the cigars, but it quickly dawned on him that the wrapping was not a laundry list, love letter, or recipe for cookies.

So the order sheet quickly raced up the Yankee chain of command until it reached a dazzled General McClellan. Lee, he learned from Order 191, was heading to Harper's Ferry and not, as Union General Halleck had told McClellan, to Washington. "If I don't crush Lee now," he boasted gleefully to his officers, "you may call me whatever you please." They eventually did.

For once, the usually cautious McClellan sprang into action. To Lee's surprise, the 90,000 men of McClellan's Army of the Potomac raced toward the South Mountain pass in an attempt to split the Confederate forces. Lee's army now found itself in a precarious position and could not hold the mountain.

Things took a turn for the better when Jackson captured Harper's Ferry on September 15 and rejoined Lee on the next day, only just in time. Still, Lee had but 40,000 men to face a force twice the size. In deciding to stand and fight at Sharpsburg (or Antietam Creek), with the Potomac at his back, Lee once again took big risks. Indeed, in the opening battle, the Confederates received several blows. Jackson was stalled by Union artillery, and it looked like Lee's army would be cut in two and beaten. On three different occasions, defeat loomed on the horizon. Jackson made a heroic stand at the left end. In the face of another offensive by the Federals, at the center of Lee's lines this time, the heavily outnumbered Southern troops buckled and were saved only by the timely arrival of Lee's last reserves.

In this battle, Lee took charge of the tactics instead of, as usual, leaving that to his subordinates. With great agility and daring, he concentrated and maneuvered his forces. As need arose, he moved them around like pieces on a chessboard. His tactics, leadership, and personal command in crisis were as good as his strategy and saw him through a series of close calls. McClellan, by contrast, did not keep a tight rein. He operated with typical caution and anxiety. Holding back his reserves and making piecemeal advances, he probably for-

Confederate dead gathered for burial at Antietam.

President Lincoln visiting the battlefield at Antietam, Maryland, October 3, 1862. General McClellan and fifteen staff members are in the group.

feited victory by never making use of all his soldiers at once.

At one point in the battle, Lee's son Robert and his unit, on the way back from the frontline with energy and ammunition depleted, passed Lee and his staff. Robert greeted his father, who was happy to see him well. "General, are you going to send us in again?"

"Yes, my son," Lee said with a smile. "You all must do what you can to help drive those people back."

The fighting on September 17 was perhaps the bloodiest single day of the war. Altogether, some 14,000 Confederates were casualties out of a force of 51,000 compared to 12,000 out of 75,000 Yankees. The battle ended indecisively. Both sides were equally stunned, but the percentage of casualties was certainly not in the South's favor. When even Jackson was hesitant, Lee ruled out further offensive action but stood his ground, his back precariously to the river, against any Northern resumption of attack. The next move was decided by the tide of events: Lee's army, in part weaponless and shoeless, was plagued with desertion, while McClellan was receiving large numbers of reinforcements. Without reinforcements of his own, Lee had few choices.

The two-week Maryland adventure was over as quickly as it had begun. The attempt to establish Confederate independence through military victory had failed, at least for now. Lee could repel McClellan, not destroy him. The failure was due as much to desertions in Lee's army, battle losses, and lack of reinforcements as to the unfortunate discovery of Order 191 and McClellan's prompt reaction.

So the Confederate Army turned around and started the march home. As it reached the Potomac, Lee sat on his horse in the stream watching the soldiers, wagons, and artillery cross the river and worrying over a Federal attack. But a dazed McClellan hesitated to renew the battle. When almost the last of the Confederate forces were safely across, Lee said, "Thank God." Then he rode on with his army back to Virginia.

7

High Tide: Fredericksburg and Chancellorsville

(September 1862–May 1863)

THE MARYLAND CAMPAIGN left Lee's army in disarray. Within two months he reorganized it. The last of the incompetent generals and the politicians functioning as amateur officers were transferred. The old system of divisions and brigades operating almost independently of one another was finally ended altogether. The army was now divided into two corps, one under General Longstreet, the other under General Jackson. Only Jackson, because he had the intelligence Lee trusted, was granted the right to act on his own if and when he could not remain in touch with army headquarters.

So far the Civil War had been a seesaw. First the South had fired on Northern forces. Then the North had invaded the South. Then, under Lee, the South invaded the North. Now it was the North's turn again. In October 1862, the

Federal army crossed the Potomac. It was, as usual, heavily armed, but what was different this time was the absence of McClellan. He had been replaced as Commander in Chief by General Ambrose Burnside.

Lee's 72,000 men faced a force of 106,000. The two armies converged on Fredericksburg, Virginia. Feeling no fear of his new opponent, Lee allowed Burnside to cross the Rappahannock River and to attack the strong Confederate defensive position on the other side of the town. As part of their increasing reliance on total warfare, the Federals began to shell and destroy the city. Lee was angered by this (at that time) uncommon assault on weak and defenseless civilians.

Lee established his main forces on Marye's Heights, an elevation outside the city. There he built a solid fortification line which included breastworks, stone walls, and rifle pits. To take Lee's army, Burnside had to send his men across a sunken road, over a stone wall, and up a hill. On December 13, 1862, the Federals charged no less than six times across these hurdles and right into the face of the artillery firing at them.

On came the men in blue uniforms, with their fine weapons and plentiful ammunition. Yet charge after charge succeeded only in piling up the bodies of the dead and wounded. Burnside seemed to know nothing except head-on attack, and that was not working for him. This time the Federals had 12,700 casualties, the Confederates only 5,300, most of the latter with minor wounds. Given the disparity in forces, it was a great victory for Lee, but as in the Battle of the Seven Days, he felt regret that he had not been able to follow up and destroy Burnside's army. This lapse was remarked on by other Southerners and by English

A view of Fredericksburg, Virginia, before the battle.

observers as well. Lee, it turned out, had not acted because he did not at first realize just how seriously crippled the Federal army was.

In one part of the battle of Fredericksburg, Confederate soldiers had rushed out of the woods with their famous bloodcurdling "rebel yell"—half Indian war cry, half wolf-howl: "Aah-ih!"—and routed some Federal troops. Watching this scene from a nearby hill, Lee had turned with excitement to General Longstreet and uttered his most memorable words: "It is well that war is so terrible—we should grow too fond of it!"

This remark expresses his love for and hatred of war. This is the paradox of the man, perhaps the paradox of all men. It goes with the paradox of this gentle soul giving aid and comfort to the causes of slavery and rebellion.

IN RICHMOND, optimism reached new heights. Everyone felt that the war would soon be over and the South would be officially recognized as an independent nation. After all, the North seemed to be spending itself into bankruptcy for the sake of one defeat after another, and on the New York financial exchanges Confederate bonds were, for once, as good as Federal ones.

And so, as 1862 drew to a close, Lee had much to be proud of. Of thirteen battles fought under his command in the second half of the year, eleven were victories. The Confederates had 48,000 casualties against 71,000 Federal ones. They had captured large piles of weapons and supplies. The morale of the soldiers was high.

Lee alone knew, however, that many serious problems remained. He continually wrote to Richmond warning of the effect that shortages of food and supplies for men and horses would have on troop morale and combat effectiveness. He demanded an overhaul of the railroad supply system. Yet his warnings and requests went unheeded by Davis and the Confederate politicians, who had become spoiled by Lee's successes. Seeing him as a brilliant and reliable man, they expected him to keep pulling off miracles even while they took military units away from him for use on other fronts. The irony was that the more successful Lee became, the more was he taken for granted, left on his own without aid, and, worse, the more was expected from him.

The Confederate leaders believed that Lee's needs could be subordinated to those of the other fronts—in Tennessee and Mississippi—where lesser men led. He, on the contrary, thought that the Confederacy should concentrate on the Army of Northern Virginia, the one successful army the South had. If it were sent North again into Maryland, the South could force the Federals to pull back from Tennessee and Mississippi in order to defend their capital.

In the spring of 1863, as campaigning resumed, Lincoln replaced Burnside with yet another Commander in Chief, General Joseph Hooker. The Union Army of the Potomac now had 138,000 to the Army of Northern Virginia's 62,000. What was worse, as the Federal forces approached, General Longstreet's corps was slow to join the main force, so that Lee was not even at full strength. Lee nearly always had an inferiority of numbers, but never one of such seriousness. His position was being threatened from every direction. Even so he actually planned to take the offensive.

The Federals struck first, though, and tried to make an end-run around Lee's army. Lee had to make a stand in the wilderness around Chancellorsville. This was a thick, barely penetrable forest where normal infantry and artillery maneuvers were ruled out. Here his tactics could overcome the difference in the numbers of soldiers and guns. Lee reasoned that the Southerners, precisely because Hooker expected them to retreat, should look for an opportunity to make a surprise attack at a vulnerable point.

Lee now met with Stonewall Jackson. Their mutual respect had become mutual affection. For his part, Jackson said of Lee: "He is a phenomenon. He is the only man I would follow blindfolded."

Lee informed Jackson that he had decided on a daring pincers movement. Jackson's assignment was to take his forces around the Federals' right flank on an old road

Lieutenant General Thomas Jonathan "Stonewall" Jackson shortly before his death.

through the forest and then to the enemy's rear at Chancellorsville.

"My troops will move at four o'clock," Jackson said.

"What do you propose to make this movement with?"

"With my whole corps."

Lee had thought only of a diversion by a small force that

would distract the enemy and be a prelude to a large frontal assault by Lee's main army. Lee finally said, "What will you leave me?"

"Two divisions."

That would leave Lee's already divided force divided again to face the main Northern army. If Hooker attacked while Jackson was getting into position, Lee and his mere 14,000 men would be wiped out.

But Lee liked the sheer daring of Jackson's idea, which gave the initiative to the Confederacy and thereby helped redeem the numerical inferiority. It was a high-risk venture for both men. But then the entire Confederate cause was a high-risk venture. Like other great generals, Lee preferred to dwell on the possible gains rather than on the perils.

"Well," Lee said. "Go on."

And that was that. So began one of the most famous field maneuvers in military history.

Jackson marched quickly around Hooker's right and, on May 2, 1863, fell on the Federal rear. The plan worked beautifully. The Southern troops were fresh and primed for action. The Yankee troops were eating, sleeping, playing cards. Taken by surprise, they fought a little and then ran. Once Jackson's attack began, Lee made an attack of his own in order to prevent Hooker from reinforcing the troops facing Jackson.

The joys of success were quickly soured by a personal and national disaster. As night fell, Jackson rode out on a road with his staff to study the situation. Yankee sharpshooters quickly forced them to return to their own side. Some North Carolina troops, thinking that a detachment of the enemy was crossing the road, fired at the approaching group. Jackson was hit by three bullets, one of which pierced an artery.

A messenger brought Lee the very good news of Jackson's victory and the very bad news of the wounding. He was terribly shaken. He stopped the messenger in the middle of the report because he could not bear to hear any more about what had happened. "Ah, Captain, any victory is dearly bought which deprives us of the services of General Jackson, even for a short time!" He later he wrote Jackson: "Could I have directed events, I would have chosen for the good of the country to be disabled in your stead."

Jackson was replaced by Jeb Stuart, and his forces attacked now in coordination with Lee's. The two forces joined, and Lee took personal command and led the offensive to a magnificent climax. Hooker's army, losing its way in the wilderness, was routed despite all its advantages. Lee had won a big victory. The terribly dressed, fed, and equipped, beggar-like soldiers of the South were proving to be unbeatable when facing the well-dressed, -fed, -equipped Yankees because of the way they were led. With typical modesty, the triumphant Lee, on receiving the wounded Jackson's congratulations, responded, "Say to General Jackson that the victory is his and that the congratulation is due to him."

Inside the White House, President Lincoln was utterly shocked when news reached him on May 5 of yet another Federal military disaster. He had tried various generals, he had given his generals everything they could want, and still victory eluded him in this war everyone had thought would soon be over. He walked up and down the Oval Office in great agitation, saying, "My God! My God! What will the country say? What will the country say?"

A Union artillery battery in action at Fredericksburg, May 3, 1863.

Lincoln was asking the right question. The war seemed to be going against the North, and the people there were outraged. Desertions from the Federal army increased. Civilians resisted being drafted, even to the point of rioting in New York City at the cost of hundreds of lives. Newspapers and politicians, especially the peace advocates known as the "Copperheads," declared the war to be futile and came close to recognizing the South's legitimacy. The impact of Lee's victories, in short, was being felt far beyond the battlefield.

Chancellorsville is considered one of the most brilliant of military victories, with unsurpassable strategy, tactics, and fighting. Its brilliance is the greater when one considers the differences in manpower and equipment and the great risks Lee took in twice dividing his army and still succeeding through agile maneuvers. The victory prevented the Army of the Potomac for a whole year from resuming the advance on Richmond. Still, Lee paid a high price—13,000 casualties, including many officers. Though the Federals had 17,000 casualties, their loss in percentages was far smaller, and they could in any case much better afford them.

The Confederate losses were larger even than Lee first thought. Word soon came that Fredericksburg, Virginia, the scene of a Confederate victory a few months earlier, had been captured by the Federals. This meant that Hooker could not be driven into the river. New Confederate troop movements, without Jackson's presence, were slow and awkward. Already, Jackson's absence was making itself felt. Fortunately, Hooker's army left on May 5.

Then more bad news bulletins poured in:

Jackson's left arm had to be amputated.

Jackson had come down with pneumonia.

Jackson had drifted into a coma.

Lee said, "He has lost his left arm, but I have lost my right."

Within hours, Jackson was dead.

Lee was stunned. He wept openly over the "the great and good Jackson," with face buried in his hands. No eulogy could do justice to Jackson the man and to the contribution he had made to the Confederate cause.

Now, not so coincidentally, began the long descent of Lee's military fortunes. Brilliant as he had been, his success was partly due—as he himself was the first to say—to the equal, or nearly equal, brilliance of Jackson. But Jackson was dead now. Lee would have to do the best he could on his own. He knew that things would go much harder. The bad luck of the misplaced Order 191 was nothing compared to what these North Carolina soldiers unintentionally had done in wounding Jackson. Even while Lincoln and the North were reeling under the impact of Chancellorsville, that one incident in the battle would unravel the entire Southern cause.

. There was sorrow, on this day halfway through the war, in both the North and the South. The horrors of war often rain equally on all sides. Yet there was a difference. For Lincoln, the bad news on this day was almost the last in a long series of such bulletins. For Lee it was the beginning.

8

The Turning Point: Gettysburg

(*May–July 1863*)

THE CASUALTIES of war were brought home to Lee in another intimate form. His son, General W. H. F. "Rooney" Lee, was wounded in action one month after Chancellorsville. Lee saw the young man being carried to the rear, and he hoped—so he wrote his wife—that their son would soon recover. Rooney was taken to a country home for recuperation, where there followed a further blow to Lee: Rooney was seized by a Federal raiding party sent out just for this purpose. He was to be held as a hostage in return for some Union officers. Almost a year passed before he was exchanged. Lee refused to ask for any special consideration for his son.

These personal setbacks reached tragic proportions as Rooney's sick wife became terminally ill. Lee's son Custis offered himself as a substitute hostage so that Rooney could spend his wife's last days with her. The offer was refused. Rooney's wife died before he was released, and it was some time before he was ready to resume his military duties.

THE CATASTROPHIC DEATH of Jackson called for immediate reorganization. Lee could not continue doing things as in the past. Jackson had been such a big man militarily that it took two men to fill his shoes, and they did poorly at that. His corps was divided in half, and the men appointed new corps commanders were the best Lee could find, but they were nowhere near what the times required. One, A. P. Hill, was inexperienced, and the other, Richard Ewell, was indecisive. Further reorganization brought in new officers who did not know the veteran soldiers they had to lead or Lee's methods they had to follow. Those weaknesses were to have severe consequences in battles yet to come.

Now that the Federal invasion of Virginia in the wake of Lee's invasion of Maryland had been blocked, it was the South's turn again. The pendulum swung once more in the direction of a Confederate invasion of the North.

Federal forces were making serious inroads on all other fronts of the war—in Mississippi, Tennessee, North Carolina, and eastern Virginia. The best way, Lee always maintained, to relieve the embattled Confederate forces in these places was to hit the enemy hard on the main front in northern Virginia and near the enemy's capital. Lee was therefore eager to invade Pennsylvania. A daring thrust there would bring the surprised Federal forces racing northward, exhausted and demoralized, they would be crushed by him piecemeal.

A second reason for the foray was that Pennsylvania, unlike ravaged Virginia, was rich in provisions for his hungry army. A third reason was to give the Northern civilians another taste of war. That would help the growing peace movement there and neutralize the moral effect of Lincoln's Emancipation Proclamation. A quick victory on Union soil as a follow-up to the smashing victory at Chancellorsville would have a definitive effect on morale in North and South. If it also finally brought European opinion around to the South, it might well end the war and establish Southern independence.

Just before the invasion began, in the late spring of 1863, Lee wrote President Davis a letter criticizing the Confederacy again for its continuing policy of defending all its territories rather than going on the offensive. He warned that the resources of the North, with its seemingly infinite reserves, were growing while those of the South, especially the Army of Northern Virginia, were shrinking. The North could simply wait it out and grind down the South slowly. Time was running out. Defeat could be averted only by fighting at places and times the South selected, that is, by the offensive. That was the point of invading Pennsylvania.

Along with this military strategy there had to be an encouragement of the peace party in the North. Lee was sure that once peace talks began, the North would rather settle for peace at the cost of Southern independence than face a resumption of combat. He was also sure that the South, despite all the initial enthusiasm for the war, would be willing to make peace at the cost of rejoining the Union. With both sides exhausted by two years of fighting and willing to make concessions that were unthinkable before, there were good grounds for holding peace talks soon. The only way the situation could be exploited by men seeking peace would be to accept, without preconditions, any offers to begin peace talks. The terms of a settlement (that is, Southern independence) could be worked out in the negotiating process and should not be allowed to prevent such a process from beginning.

President Davis ignored the ideas in the letter. Still the amateur general, he had his own ideas about the Confederate strategy. He thought that Lee knew well only the one front he was bogged down in, while Davis had the whole war to run. In a way that was true, except that what Lee was bogged down in was the main front. If he fell, all fell; if he won, all won.

Davis's strategy was to defend the South everywhere. He therefore wanted Lee to hand over troops to help in the campaigns in Tennessee and Mississippi. Lee, for his part, believed that trying to defend everything would stretch out the meager Confederate resources and result in defeat everywhere. Far better to have, even at the cost of a temporary loss of this or that part of the Confederacy, a single concentrated force free to maneuver, to take the offensive wherever and whenever the enemy exposed a weak flank. Lee would have taken troops wasted in a defensive position around Richmond and in the far-flung fronts of the Confederacy and used them to threaten Washington and put the Northern army on the defensive. He had a hard time persuading the Richmond officials, and only when he bluntly offered them the choice of losing Mississippi or Virginia did they back away reluctantly from their requests for troops for the Deep South.

The result was that in any new invasion of the North, Lee would be without much help or encouragement from the Confederate government. On top of which, he was still recovering from the effects of the loss of Jackson. Unlike a year earlier, this time when he planned to attack on enemy soil, he was without Jackson performing brilliantly at his side and without Davis wholeheartedly behind him. Lee can be forgiven for not having had the enthusiasm for this offensive that he had a year earlier on entering Maryland.

So began on June 25, 1863, the second Southern invasion of the North, the South's last and greatest effort to win independence through offensive action. Lee insisted that his troops act decently. Private property was to be respected, and all foods and materiel were to be duly paid for—although in Confederate money. Of course, Lee's scrupulous orders in these matters were not always carried out by his men.

Meanwhile, the North had yet another command change, as General George Meade replaced Hooker. For once, the two armies were almost numerically equal, but things soon began to sour for the invaders. Lee lost contact with Jeb Stuart's cavalry. This was a serious development. Stuart's force, with its daring raids, always provided him with important intelligence information. He had called Stuart the "eyes of the army."

The trouble was that Stuart, ever something of a showoff, had allowed himself to be distracted by a sideshow. He could not resist making a raid on a tempting train of 150 horse wagons. It was a great feat, it brought pleasure and glory to him, but it disrupted all coordination in the Southern army. This was simply not the time or place for such an unauthorized foray, however dashing and successful. It left Lee moving blindly into enemy territory. He did not know that Meade had successfully concentrated his forces, and he was dangerously unaware of the exact location of the Federal army. Stuart's absence caused Lee to stumble into battle at Gettysburg without foresight and against his will. Neither Lee nor Meade had had any plans to fight at that place and at that time.

Another growing problem was that the new organization of the Second Corps was not working well. General Ewell became emotionally paralyzed in a crisis. Longstreet, as

A view of Gettysburg from Cemetery Ridge with Seminary Ridge in the left background. A Union Army encampment is at right center.

usual, moved too slowly. At Second Manassas he had similarly procrastinated, but there Jackson had kept back the enemy for two days. Here there was no Jackson to redeem Longstreet's lapses.

The first day of fighting, on July 1, resulted when detachments from each side stumbled into one another and both sides began rushing reinforcements against what they thought was the main enemy force. The Confederates captured Seminary Ridge, the Federals Cemetery Ridge. The Confederates had the upper hand. Much more could have been achieved, though, if General Ewell had been up to the pursuit of the fleeing Yankees that Lee urged on him. Lee, as often, did not order, and Ewell therefore did not move. Still, the Confederates had won, their troops were enthusiastic, and Lee believed—mistakenly, in the absence of Stuart and his reconnaissance information—that Meade had only a part of the army with him.

Both sides raced to concentrate their forces for the resumption of the unavoidable battle; retreat was impossible. On the next day, things started to become sticky for Lee. What happened that day and the next would make for great comedy were it not that men's lives and suffering were at stake. There was a breakdown in coordination, and Longstreet became a real problem. At one planning session, Lee had indicated his desire that Longstreet and his First Corps come quickly to the attack. He did not actually order Longstreet to do so. Longstreet had ideas of his own as to how to plot this campaign. He wanted to use defensive tactics in the midst of the offensive strategy of this invasion, while Lee wanted offensive tactics. Longstreet stuck to his ideas even after Lee established his plan. When Lee listened politely to

Longstreet's ideas without rejecting them, Longstreet thought, or pretended, that Lee had agreed to let him follow his own ideas. Lee was placing too much responsibility on the only corps commander with experience and, for once, too much trust in a man he did not fully know. If Lee's other subordinate generals were losing their nerve, Longstreet was losing his head.

Various actions and movements, in the intricate design or ballet that is a battle plan, were dependent on Longstreet, and so when he failed to show up where he was supposed to, Lee's careful planning came apart. Longstreet was to attack at dawn but did not do so until 4 P.M. He wanted to wait for all forces to be coordinated before striking, while Lee was worried by the delay. In the time that was lost, Federal reinforcements arrived.

Finally, an exasperated Lee ordered Longstreet to attack, but Longstreet still took his time. Then another general suggested to Longstreet a way to modify the battle plan because of changed battle conditions. But Longstreet, after having opposed Lee's strategy and having dragged his feet in carrying it out, now had the gall to stick to the exact details of Lee's plan. Unimaginatively insisting on the letter rather than the spirit of Lee's strategy, Longstreet was being petulant and childish. Junior officers told Longstreet that if Lee knew of how things had changed in the last hours, how heavily reinforced the Yankee positions were, he would call off the attack, but Longstreet did not bother to inform Lee of these facts.

In spite of all this, Federal losses were huge, the Confederates seemed close to splitting the Federal army, and Meade almost ordered a general Federal retreat that night.

Lieutenant General James Longstreet.

The third day of battle began full of promise. Lee found that he still had enough troops on hand. Stuart at long last showed up with his forces. Longstreet was reinforced with George Pickett's division. Lee had planned on a concerted attack early in the morning. But now things started to fall apart.

The Federals attacked first and knocked Ewell, who did not receive proper support, out of the day's fighting. Longstreet was supposed to order a bombardment at a crucial hour, but, still unwilling to attack, he tried to pass the responsibility for the decision to an underling.

Finally, the Confederate cannons fired, and a terrible artillery duel broke out, perhaps the biggest in history until that day. The Confederate artillery commander urged Pickett to send in the infantry before he himself ran out of the ammunition needed to provide protective cover for the foot soldiers. Pickett asked Longstreet whether to charge now. Longstreet said nothing and just barely nodded or shook his head. It was Lee's idea to have this charge, not Longstreet's, and he just could not bring himself to give his approval. A

Confederate dead at Gettysburg. The corpses are shoeless, because the survivors needed them.

little later, Longstreet, declaring his own inability to launch an attack that he did not believe would succeed, wanted Pickett to stop the advance.

It was too late. The most famous military charge in the history of the American continent was under way. Pickett's division—forty-two regiments of soldiers in their pitifully tattered Confederate gray or butternut colored uniforms—charged across the field and up the slope of the aptly named Cemetery Ridge. There the men in their smart blue uniforms crouched behind their entrenchments and nervously held their fire until the enemy was quite close. The July sun beat down on everyone in the afternoon heat and dust. Going up the slope on such a day would have been tough even for a picnic, but still the brave Confederates came closer and closer. And still the Federal officers waited.

Then came that long awaited, or dreaded, word . . . "Fire!" And all hell broke loose.

The Confederate infantrymen showed great heroism under the withering fusillade. They kept on going as men fell to the left and to the right of them. They even managed, some of them, to reach the Federal lines but could not break through. Without proper support, they were simply butchered.

It was all in vain, all that planning by Lee and all that effort by the foot soldiers. The breakdown in coordination among the Confederates was complete. Other forces that were supposed to move in concert with Pickett's did not. Of nine divisions, seven did nothing at all, while two bore the brunt of the enemy's fire. It turned into a horrible massacre, into a disaster worthy of a General Pope or Burnside. Only a third of Pickett's men returned. A terribly distraught Lee on horseback met them, repeating agonizingly, "It is all my fault."

Lee later said that if he had known of the absence of sufficient artillery ammunition, he would have cancelled the charge. Instead of blaming those officers responsible for not keeping him informed, he characteristically said to Pickett, "Upon my shoulders rests the blame."

In a report after the battle, Pickett complained of lack of support on that grim day. Years later, when the retired, aging Lee was touring the South, an uncomfortable Pickett, who was to have a run-in with Lee in the closing days of the war, reluctantly paid him a brief social call. They were cold to each other, and, when Pickett emerged, he referred to Lee bitterly as "that old man," adding, "He had my division massacred at Gettysburg." Pickett was one of the very few people who had unkind things to say of Lee.

Gettysburg—the greatest, bloodiest, most important and decisive battle of the war—is famous not only because of Lincoln's eloquent speech. It was the sorry climax to a series of unhappy events that suggested that Lee had passed the zenith of his career and was now on a downward course. He had begun the invasion halfheartedly because of lack of support from the government. Then he had been disoriented by Stuart's inexcusable absence. Next, during one battle, victory slipped from him because of Ewell's inability to take action. And on the two climactic days, Longstreet had kept him waiting and thrown everything off balance, with the result that the battle was lost while plentiful reserves were unused.

Lee's judgment might not have been as sharp as it had been at Chancellorsville. Instead of the great and reliable

Jackson, he had had to work with the defective Stuart, Ewell, and Longstreet. All this must have affected a Lee who was tired and overburdened. Or had he, because of his many victories, grown too complacent about, or contemptuous of, the Yankees?

Many things had gone wrong, many generals had been slow or irresponsible or nearly insubordinate, but Lee blamed no one. To a general whose apologetic, explanatory words were halted as he was overcome by weeping, Lee said, "Never mind, General, all this has been my fault—it is I that have lost this fight." As always he was too ready to accept the excuses of incompetent officers. He showed no resentment, made no criticism, blamed no one else. He thought that he had expected too much from his army.

And, in a way, he was right, and it was his fault. It is the job of a leader to assess correctly how far he can go with the men at his disposal and to take into account their limitations. It was Lee's task to know Longstreet, to push Longstreet and Ewell, to make sure he got all the necessary information, and to get the best out of his officers and men. No doubt Lee would not have made these errors if he had had better officers and officers he knew better. Years later, in one of his few glances back, Lee said sadly, "If I had had Stonewall Jackson with me . . . I should have won the battle of Gettysburg."

Later, on that fateful night of July 3, Lee was riding alone on his horse in the bright moonlight. He was returning to his headquarters tent after having surveyed the state of his army, having watched and heard the sufferings of his wounded, the utter exhaustion of his remaining combat-ready soldiers in the stifling nighttime heat. He dismounted with difficulty, even had to be helped down, and then leaned against the horse. The moon highlighted, to assistants and attendants, his expression of extreme sadness and grief.

Finally, he said, "I never saw troops behave more magnificently than Pickett's Virginians did today in that grand charge. . . . And if they had been supported as they were to have been . . . the day would have been ours. Victory might have led to an attack on Washington." Then he stared into the darkness as a last heartbreaking few words came out: "Too bad! . . . Too bad! . . . Oh, too bad!"

Food and ammunition were low; a third of the soldiers were not combat-ready. Once again the Confederate army had to trudge home from Northern soil with dreams unfulfilled. The march home was bitter, the more so as it took place in days of terrible unending rain. The roads were ponds, no shelter was available, the Potomac was flooding. As the rains kept the army away from Virginia longer than had been expected, there was the fear, even expectation, of a Northern attack at this bad time. The methods that had worked with Jackson, of giving him semi-independent command, had failed badly at Gettysburg without Jackson's presence. So now, on the retreat, Lee gave precise orders and left no room for modification.

No attack, though, took place. The Northern forces were as shell-shocked as the Southern ones. When Meade finally, on July 14, was able to organize for pursuit of the retreating Southerners, Lee had gotten them across the Potomac. Lee was greatly relieved when the last troops crossed the bridge. He had managed to carry with him his wounded, his prisoners, and most of his artillery. As the famous British statesman and historian Winston Churchill put it so poignantly: "He had lost only two guns, and the war."

9

Against the Tide: The Wilderness and Spotsylvania

(July 1863–May 1864)

WHEN THE ARMY came back to Confederate soil, there was disappointment throughout the South. Lee's successes had caused expectations to soar out of control. After Lee had pushed Federal forces out of Virginia and the Shenandoah Valley, disrupted the Federal campaign for the summer, and relieved pressures on the Atlantic coast forces, this was quite a letdown. Criticism of the supposedly invincible Lee's failed campaign could be heard in the Richmond government and press. As Lee humorously put it, when war broke out, "We appointed all our worst generals to command our armies, and all our best generals to edit the newspapers."

With the soldiers, Lee remained as popular as ever. Nevertheless, he asked, on August 8, 1863, to be relieved of his command. President Davis would not hear of it. Where could he find a replacement? A man "more fit to command"

and possessing "more of the confidence of the Army" did not exist.

The psychological depression in the South was deepened by other bad news. On July 4, the very day after the Battle of Gettysburg and the beginning of Lee's sad march home, General Ulysses S. Grant captured Vicksburg on the western front, thus bringing the Confederate West and the Mississippi River into Federal control and freeing his army for operations elsewhere. The Confederacy had reached a low point in its fortunes. And the destiny of Grant was rising at the very time that Lee's was starting its decline. The two men would soon meet on the field of combat, but on terribly uneven terms.

Recovery from the Pennsylvania campaign was difficult. Though within a month Lee was able to bring his strength back to 58,000 combat-ready men, the army was hobbled by chronic shortages. Food, shoes, and blankets were, as always, in great demand. Lack of food for the horses also crippled the army's mobility. Replacements of men were hard to obtain, and a shortage of good officers developed as well. The Army of Northern Virginia was plainly no longer what it had been.

If 1862 had turned out, after a slow start, to be a great year for Lee, 1863 was turning out, after a great start, to be a poor year. Instead of a repetition of triumphs such as Chancellorsville, there had come the difficulties of Gettysburg and thereafter. The war was going badly for the South on all fronts except—thanks to Lee—on Lee's, yet even that front was in peril because he had an uphill struggle getting his own government to confront the problems he faced.

He asked again, as he had in the past, that nearly all

able-bodied men be drafted into the army. The Congress was slow in coming to see things his way. In vain did he urge again that forces be concentrated to fight the Federal Army of the Potomac on the main front. In vain did he also warn the government that if something was not done about the scandalous supply system—or nonsystem—both the capital, Richmond, and the Confederate cause would go down. In later years, he complained that the terrible failure of the Commissary (Supply) Department to provide food and materiel caused him more trouble than any other aspect of the war, more even than the enemy.

During the rest of 1863, there was a lot of moving about of forces and of skirmishing, as neither Lee nor Meade wanted to, or could, bring the other to a major battle. The winter of 1863–1864 was an especially difficult time for Lee and his men. A Southerner, especially a Virginian, and above all the husband of a descendant of George Washington, could well be pardoned for thinking of Valley Forge and an earlier justified rebellion. Lee's General Order of January 22, 1864 said, "Soldiers! You tread with no unequal step the road by which your fathers marched through suffering, privations, and blood, to independence." And as bad as 1863 became, it was nothing compared to 1864. As the war dragged on, the Federals resorted more and more to total war. Lee, outraged by this ruthlessness, refused to be drawn into retaliation.

In March 1864, Lincoln made several major moves. He called for the drafting of 700,000 men—this at a time when the Army of Northern Virginia had one tenth of that number and could hardly get any additions at all. And he made Grant Commander in Chief of the Army of the Potomac.

Lieutenant General Ulysses S. Grant at Cold Harbor, Virginia, June 1864.

That job had certainly seen a high turnover of personnel. In a way, Lee was like a heavyweight boxing champion who knocked out one contender after another. First and lasting the longest was McClellan, a very good administrator and planner but much too cautious militarily and ambitious politically. Then there had come in quick succession the mediocre Irvin McDowell; the boastful, ruthless, but ignorant Pope; the unassuming, ineffective Burnside; the hard-drinking showoff Hooker; the competent but outclassed

Meade. Because of the genius at the head of the impover-
ished army they confronted, none of these men had been
able to have any success leading the most massive, best
equipped army ever to appear in the Western hemisphere.

Now Lincoln had finally found himself a man with con-
siderable military skills. U.S. ("Unconditional Surrender"
was the nickname the officers gave him) Grant was probably
not in Lee's league either as a human being or as a military
thinker, but he was much better than his predecessors. He
had daring and military intelligence and persistence; he had
a record of winning battles against Southern forces; he and
Lincoln saw eye-to-eye. With over a half million men under
his command, Grant was given greater powers than any
general on either side had had.

That Grant, unlike his predecessors, finally beat Lee is
due not to Grant's being a better general but to some simple
facts. Lee's army was running out of everything, while
Grant's army was growing. Grant had, moreover, supreme
command over all Federal forces and could obtain reinforcements from other fronts whenever he needed them, whereas
Lee commanded only his own army and could only request
reinforcements from Davis, usually in vain. Grant also had
strong support. Because of the political pressures in Washington, the earlier generals worked under the unwritten rule
of "One defeat and you're fired." Grant took his beatings
from Lee like the rest, but Lincoln sensed he had his man
at last, and the old rule was suspended.

And Grant did have the virtue of persistence. Under the
other Federal generals in Virginia, a setback in one sector
during a battle seemed to be followed by a collapse of the
entire line. Not so with Grant. Things looked grim for Lee.

On May 4, 1864, General Grant began his campaign, the one that finally ended the war. He had a force of 125,000 as against Lee's 65,000. But he started badly. He marched his main army on the shortest route to Richmond, which happened to lead right through the wilderness of Spotsylvania. This was the forest in which Hooker had gotten entangled and smashed exactly one year before and in which their artillery would be less useful to the Federals. Lee was surprised, pleasantly, that Grant would be so foolish as to repeat Hooker's error and "throw away . . . the immense advantage which his great superiority in numbers gave him."

For his part, Grant was not afraid of Lee's reputation and was spoiling for a fight. Although some of the older officers of the Army of the Potomac predicted that Grant would find beating Lee not as easy as beating the Confederate generals in the West had been, Grant had several advantages his predecessors lacked: President Davis listened little to Lee nowadays and was less of a support to the Virginian; and Grant had working with him a cavalry general, Philip Sheridan, as bold as Jeb Stuart was on the other side. Sheridan's forces, far superior in numbers and equipment to those of Stuart, made raids on Richmond in order to keep Stuart, Lee's "eyes," away from the main force.

Lee realized that this was a do-or-die campaign. In 1863 in the wilderness, he had had reserves of men and food which he did not now have. Then he had been on the advance; now he had to act defensively. Yet army morale was as high as ever, and Lee was able to go on the offensive in that wilderness so well known to him and unknown to Grant.

On May 6, the armies lunged at each other, in the thick woods, where they could hardly see; 200,000 men met, as a contemporary witness said, in the "bloodiest and weirdest of encounters. War had had nothing like it." Some half-dozen attacks were made in vain, and Grant was halted in the wilderness. He would find his success, it now became clear, through sheer numbers rather than strategy and maneuver. And indeed, on the next day, as Longstreet was again hampering the effort with his slow movement, the Southerners had to yield to the intense Northern pressure.

At one point, Lee intervened and proposed to go at the head of his soldiers in a counterattack. Ever beloved, he was yelled at by his men, "Go back, General Lee! Go back! ... We won't go on unless you go back!" They seized his horse and insisted on leading him away from danger. When this happened a second time somewhat later, Lee answered, "If you will promise me to drive those people from our works [fortifications], I will go back."

The soldiers kept their promise. Southern counterattacks finally forced the Yankees to retreat. Grant or no Grant, the Army of the Potomac had once more been outmaneuvered by the Army of Northern Virginia. Fighting continued into the night. Then fire started to rage out of control in the woods. Together with the thick smoke, it prevented the wounded from being attended to. Grant himself was completely unnerved by this nightmare. For a while, he threw himself on his bed face down, unable to function. As someone put it, Grant and his hammer had met Lee and his rapier.

It was another of Lee's military masterpieces. Against overwhelming odds, he had kept the enemy at bay and counterattacked while the two halves of his army were separated. Grant and his officers made many mistakes and suff-

ered in two days 14,000 casualties as against 8,000 Confederate ones. The famous Grant, the North's best card, was
losing men on the scale of Burnside at Fredericksburg and
Hooker at Chancellorsville. Lee came to believe that a few
more battles like this would finally bring the North to the
peace table.

It was too good to be true, and sure enough bad news
quickly mingled with good. Despite a tactical victory, Lee
did not have the men and the officers to follow through and
take the initiative. In the midst of a Southern advance, Longstreet was wounded—like Jackson, accidentally, by his own
men. Other Confederate generals fell too. The momentum
of the Southerners was halted.

Where Burnside, Hooker, and the rest withdrew in the
wake of defeat and in the face of disaster, Grant did not. Lee,
as usual able to read his opponent's mind, correctly predicted that instead of retreating, Grant would move on to
his best strategic point, Spotsylvania Courthouse. Lee therefore sent some of his own forces from the wilderness to
Spotsylvania and halted Grant there. Grant wrote to Washington the famous line: "I propose to fight it out on this line
if it takes all summer."

It did. And all the other seasons of the year as well.

Grant's shift to Spotsylvania was actually the beginning
of a series of moves in a southeasterly direction that bypassed
Richmond but finished off the South. Lee followed Grant
as if he were his shadow and fought with him until there was
little left of the Army of Northern Virginia. It was a game
of fight and run, run and fight.

Lee had to change his strategy now. His losses prevented
continuation of his agile maneuvering and mobility. Defen-

sive siege operations were called for instead. He drew on his engineering background to compensate for Grant's far larger army by building elaborate field fortifications. The Civil War had entered its third and final phase for the South. Long ago, after a year of being on the defensive to gather strength, the main Confederate army under the new leadership of Lee had tried for two years to seek a decision through a war of aggression and mobility. And now, with depleted resources, it was back on the defensive, this time in a sort of early "trench war," a new development in the history of combat. All Lee could do at this time was to delay a decision as long as possible, with the slender hope that the North would give up a task too difficult, expensive, and protracted.

At Spotsylvania, the Federals again attacked. For nearly two weeks in May there took place a preview of World War I-style fighting from trenches. The wounded and the dead lay between the lines, and, in another "modern" innovation, Grant did away with the tradition of having a truce during which the wounded were cared for and the dead were buried. This was war with no holds barred.

The Confederates were not only able to repel the Federal forces, but to inflict heavy losses on the attackers. Some of the worst fighting of the war occurred for twenty hours on May 12 in a part of the fortifications Lee had had built, that came to be called "The Bloody Angle." The Federals suffered three times the losses that the Confederates did but could afford to keep right on coming as if unhurt. Grant did not need to count the casualties. The Southern losses of 10,000, on the other hand, weighed heavily on the smaller army, particularly the losses among officers.

One of the most painful of these to Lee was the death of

cavalry General Jeb Stuart, just a year after the death of Jackson. It came right after another glorious Southern feat of arms, as Stuart's 1,100 men stopped Sheridan's 7,000. While he had his defects, the dashing Stuart had played an important role by keeping army morale high with his daring adventures and by supplying Lee with intelligence information. His absence further limited the scope of Lee's campaign.

Many of Lee's generals were dead, injured, or ill. Relations with Davis were sinking even further. In these closing months of the war, Lee was becoming a lonely man.

All told, some twenty battles in early May left Grant with casualties of 33,000 (or 2,000 men a day), Lee with 20,000. Grant was receiving large reinforcements, Lee hardly any. Davis, still not seeing, as both Grant and Lee did, that the war would be decided by the two major armies in Virginia, was reluctant to bring in men from other fronts. For a while, cavalry raids by Sheridan cut off all supplies from Richmond.

With an addition of 30,000 fresh troops, Grant maneuvered his army into new positions. Lee in turn moved his army away from Spotsylvania Courthouse to the North Anna River. It was as brilliant a stroke as the shift from the wilderness to Spotsylvania. In this late campaign of the war, Lee was as great as ever, continually able to anticipate Grant and block his access to Richmond. When asked after the war who was the best Federal general he had fought, Lee said promptly and emphatically, "McClellan, by all odds."

In fact, in a fine tactical move at one point, Lee again outwitted Grant so badly that he caught the Federal army dangerously divided on either side of the North Anna River.

Unfortunately, Lee fell ill just then and had to carry on from bed and tent so Grant got away unscathed. Lee keenly felt that his illness and the loss of his trusted generals allowed a chance to destroy Grant to slip away.

"We must strike them a blow," he exclaimed. "We must never let them pass us again! . . . If I can get one more pull at him, I will defeat him."

10

Dangerous Stalemate: Cold Harbor and the Siege Line

(May 1864–March 1865)

THOUGH BETTER than his predecessors, Grant shared in their defective strategic sense. Because he could afford it, he allowed this to become a war of attrition, that is, rubbing, wearing down. It was a brutal, mindless type of warfare, but since the North did not have generals who could use maneuver and strategy to win—did not have a Lee—it had finally to resort to this.

Grant's strategy was to throw everything he had at the enemy by the most direct route and then wait for the unending stream of replacements and supplies. Lee had no such luxuries. Fighting against great odds and without hope of reinforcements, he could only improvise. Yet, though he had an army half the size of the enemy's 100,000 men, he was able to inflict double the casualties.

Given the incredibly poor physical condition of his sol-

General Grant (bending over the bench) discussing strategy with General Meade (with map) and his other officers near Massaponax Church, Virginia, May 21, 1864.

diers and the incredible uncooperativeness of his government, Lee's generalship in 1864–1865 may well be the climax of his military career even as he drifted toward defeat. As one military historian puts it, in the campaign of 1862, Lee had shown how genius can overcome numerical inferiority even on the offensive; in the campaign of 1864–1865, he showed his ability in defensive strategy and tactics.

The Old South was probably doomed from the beginning of the war. The wonder is not that it lost but that it held out such a long time. The credit for postponing doom, for going from one victory that led nowhere to another, belongs to the military leadership and tenacity of Lee.

LEE WAS ABLE to prevent Grant from making a direct attack on Richmond. In the process he was brought back to the area, only nine miles from the capital, where he had first assumed command of the army two years earlier and where the Confederates had won The Battle of the Seven Days against McClellan. How different thing were now! In this new phase, he had only a thin line of soldiers between Grant's army and Richmond, with no reserve forces and no materiel for mounting an offensive.

On June 1, 1864, Grant started a new attack at Cold Harbor. He would give it his all. He had the whole of his 120,000 man army concentrated for one final attempt to wipe out Lee. He would finally do what McClellan and McDowell and Pope and Burnside and Hooker and Meade had failed to do.

But Grant ignored the fact that it was still Lee he was up against, not one of those Confederate generals he had beaten so easily in the West. The Federals made no less than fourteen attacks, yet the main battle was over within one hour. Casualties were some 7,000 Federals to only 1,500 Confederates—a record even for *that* bloody war. The Yankee corpses and wounded simply piled up. Aided by Northern blindness and stubbornness no less than by Lee's leadership, the defense had one of its easiest victories.

Finally, when the order for yet another attack was given,

Union Army wagon trains cross the James River.

there was no movement. The Union soldiers had had enough. They refused to march into the slaughter pen. This was serious business—mutiny. Grant had more than met his match. Like his predecessors, he had discovered in one very long month what it meant to challenge this nearly invincible general and his nearly superhuman soldiers.

The battle of Cold Harbor was one of the bloodiest yet, with some 13,000 Federal casualties all told. Grant came to regret this fight more than any other. The Federal offensives had come to a bloody, unsatisfactory climax. Northern troop morale ruled out further attack. The terrible news

from the battlefield was being increasingly censored or suppressed. The will of the people in the North, like that of the Army of the Potomac, was nearly exhausted. Some 8,000 Federal soldiers surrendered in a two-month period in the summer of 1864. The war seemed to be grinding down into a permanent stalemate.

Grant wanted to avoid another head-on collision with Lee, whose troops' morale was fine despite the shrinking of his army. On June 13, Grant pulled his army back, only to reappear a few days later at the James River. Lee had feared such a development. He had tried in vain to destroy Grant's army and to avoid being pinned down by it in the entrenchments in front of Richmond and Petersburg. Once the Federals reached the James River, Lee had predicted, it would become a siege, "and then it will be a mere question of time." But now Lee had no choice. He could not stop the Union tide, and Grant's whole army managed to cross the river. Grant then raced to Petersburg as a way of getting at Richmond. But Lee anticipated him, repulsed him, and, on the next day, directed his army to move into the defenses around the two cities. A siege line of entrenchments or earthworks, thirty-six miles long and running north and south, shielded both Richmond and Petersburg. Grant's offensives and maneuvering against Lee's army were over, and so was Lee's campaigning in the field.

Combat died down in the rest of the year. Since May 1, Grant had lost 60,000 men—as many as were in Lee's entire army!—to Lee's 25,000. Grant had finally found a formula for victory: Do nothing. Having failed to destroy Lee through hammer blows, he would let time and hunger, rather than Northern troops, do their work through a siege of the two cities. This was slow, grim, unimaginative war. Lee scorned Grant as a man whose talent lay solely in "accumulating overwhelming numbers." But Lee could no longer do anything about that.

From late June 1864 onward, Grant's strategy consisted of making forays here and there along the long trenches manned by a thin line of Confederate troops. These resulted in sporadic flare-ups of short, fierce, but inconclusive fighting rather than large set battles. For Lee it was now literally a "last-ditch stand." When a politician asked him what reserve forces he had in case Grant broke through, he answered that he had none at all. "If I shorten my lines to provide a reserve, he will turn me [at the flanks]; if I weaken my lines to provide a reserve, he will break me."

All Lee could do was wait. Many of the experienced officers had been killed or disabled, and only Lee and the foot soldiers remained of the original Army of Northern Virginia that had won the historic battles. But even here there were problems. Morale was declining. Food was down to two days' ration. The desertion rate rose. Sherman's rampage through Georgia, destroying farms and towns, put pressure on Lee to withdraw troops from his own front. Lee himself was wearing out; physical illness was becoming a semi-permanent state for him. All the while, Grant's army grew in strength. Lee began to speak in private letters to government officials of the inevitable end in the face of the enemy's vast and growing superiority, of the possible fall of Richmond, of impending "disaster"—words he had never used before.

The only "battle" was on July 30. Grant had been told that direct assault could not break through Lee's entrenchments. He was therefore willing to try something unusual. Some of his engineers built tunnels under one part of the line and filled them with explosives. When the experiment was ready, the fuse was lit—and nothing happened. Two volunteers went in and discovered that the fuse had gone out. They re-lit it and rushed out.

Finally, an explosion took place. The earth trembled, a gigantic mass of red flames and a mushroom cloud rose. In place of that part of the fortification there was now a huge crater two hundred feet long, fifty feet wide, thirty feet deep. Federal troops, readied for the explosion, went into action and then disappeared in the crater. The dead and the wounded were mixed up in the loose soil, and a short savage fight broke out there. When it was over, no major change had taken place.

The "Battle of the Crater" was a successful Confederate repulse; another 4,000 Yankees were out of action. It was Grant's last attempt to break the lines. This battle also saw the first use of blacks as soldiers by the North, which only served to enrage the Confederates; their savage treatment of the Northern black soldiers was, according to one Southern eyewitness, "sickening."

In early September 1864, Sherman seized Atlanta. The fall of Georgia came just in time to help Lincoln rout the Democrats, with their peace program, at the election polls in November. Instead of the demoralization that covered the North earlier that year, Lincoln now had a mandate to carry the war through to the bitter end. An unofficial peace conference held on neutral soil in Canada came to nothing. New Federal armies were to be formed out of the large number of drafted men. The South was to get peace only on the North's terms.

In the face of these developments, President Davis and the Confederate Congress more and more lost contact with reality. They regarded the fall of Georgia as a bearable military setback and ignored the political momentum it provided Lincoln. They hardly realized that, in a sense, only Lee, with his genius, determination, sense of duty, and the army he had shaped himself, stood between the South and the bitter end. His defensive trenches, with their line of poorly supplied troops stretched from Richmond to Petersburg, was all that was left of the secession and the second war of independence. They looked to Lee to continue to work miracles and did not bother to provide the material to work them with. By not paying or feeding his soldiers, as well as by their poor enforcement of the conscription (draft) act, they were actually encouraging desertion. When Lee tried in person to inform the Confederate Congress of army conditions, he came away depressed: "They don't seem to be able to do anything except eat peanuts and chew tobacco, while my army is starving."

Now Grant took a further step in the war of attrition. He stopped the old military tradition of exchanging prisoners of war. That move had the effect of depriving the South of living, healthy soldiers—a captured rebel was as good as a dead one. At the same time, the Northern prisoners of war in Southern hands were just more mouths to feed in a time and place with little enough food available even for the Confederate soldiers. At the same time, Sheridan began a systematic destruction of the countryside to deprive both the civilians in Richmond and Petersburg and the soldiers defending them of all food.

On September 30, coordination among Lee's troops in a minor action broke down as never before. The difference in size between Northern and Southern forces continued to grow by leaps and bounds. Yet observers noted that through all this, Lee's face revealed no anxiety. He seemed hopeful of success and was an encouragement to all who saw him. In a letter written in the middle of the war, he had said, "I have no fear of the result. We may be annihilated, but we cannot be conquered." This stage of the war turned Lee, the already famous "great and good" general, into a legend.

In early 1865, as the Deep South was being carved up by other Federal armies, many politicians wanted to appoint Lee military dictator to replace Davis. Both men rejected the idea out of hand but agreed to make Lee General in Chief. It was a purely formal change, meant to soothe the critics of Davis. Preoccupied with his siege lines, Lee simply could not take on the additional responsibility of overseeing other fronts. The situation everywhere else was nearly hopeless anyway. Had he been given the post in 1862 or 1863, he might have been able to carry out his policy of concentrating everything on the main front and achieving a final decision there. Instead, the new power came to him too late and in any case it strained relations with Davis even more.

Life on the front was becoming worse. At one point, the soldiers went without almost any food for three days. During one month, desertions were as high as three thousand men, eight percent of the army. Lee again urged that all able-bodied men be drafted. He even entertained now the idea of using blacks as troops, as part of a system of "gradual emancipation." Such a drastic move was necessary if the South was to survive. The choice was hard but obvious: Would slavery "be extinguished by our enemies and the slaves used against us," or would the South give up one of its precious "social institutions" so that it could salvage its even more precious independence? The disastrous ending of a war begun over two principles would result in the sacrifice of one principle for the sake of the other. He saw that the end of slavery was inevitable and that the only question was when and by whom and how. The Confederate Congress finally passed a law drafting blacks but with no promise of emancipation.

With doom inevitable, thoughts turned to the unthinkable—surrender. Lee was perhaps willing to ask for peace at the cost of the South's having to return to the Union, but President Davis wanted Southern independence no matter what the cost. Davis, like the Confederate Congress, now lived in a dream world. Lee's task therefore was to carry on the fight to the end, because he followed duty and authority, not his private beliefs.

The choices he faced were surrender, or a suicidal fight to the end at the siege line, or a retreat to North Carolina. Of these the last seemed best. He therefore drew up a far-fetched plan for joining Johnston's army in North Carolina, together defeating Sherman's army there, and then returning together to Richmond to attack Grant. This idea looked fine on paper but ignored all the grim realities. Perhaps he knew that the plan was hopeless and merely used it to keep up everyone else's will to endure and to keep unstained Southern "honor."

Prior to withdrawing his forces from the siege line, Lee had to stun Grant's army and shorten the enemy's line to the west. And he had to do this fast, before Sheridan's cavalry fully joined Grant. A Confederate attack on March 25, 1865, at Fort Stedman at first seemed to succeed, but it soon fell apart because of poor information and weak forces. It cost 5,000 badly needed troops and actually strengthened the Federal position.

By late March, Lee's shrinking army had only 35,000 men facing Grant's growing army of 150,000. Grant was soon to be joined by Sheridan's cavalry. When two Federal armies advancing from the Deep South also joined Grant while a weak Confederate force led by Johnston joined Lee, the numbers would be a mere 280,000 to 65,000!

11

A Fateful April
Four Years Later

IT WAS APRIL of 1865. In Washington, the newly re-elected and reinaugurated President of the United States, Abraham Lincoln, conferred with advisers on the latest dispatches from the war fronts. Lincoln's face was more lined, his hair more tinged with gray, than it had been when he was first inaugurated. Yet in 1865, April seemed indeed to symbolize and celebrate the rebirth of the United States.

The North—whose cause was Federalism and emancipation—stood on the verge of victory. In only a matter of days, Lincoln would be able to announce the end of fighting. He would proclaim a new age, a spirit of reconciliation. He would at long last be able to start a peacetime presidency and govern the entire nation, as he originally had been elected to do. There were so many ideas he had for making the re-United States prosperous. Their time had come in this fateful April of 1865.

April 1: To safeguard a necessary railroad line, Lee had ordered a defense of a place called Five Forks. At first, the Confederates, outnumbered five to one, poorly clad, and weakly armed, did surprisingly well. But then, while their leading divisional officers (including Pickett of Gettysburg fame) were preoccupied with a fish cookout, they were overwhelmed by a surprise follow-up attack by Sheridan. Lee lost at least another 3,000 men, his last reserves, an important strategic position, and any lingering hope of saving Richmond. What was worse, Lee, instead of observing the battle and trying to influence its course, for once learned to his shock about it after it had happened. Pickett, who had been given the task of stopping Sheridan, simply dared not tell Lee the truth. With the line now broken, Lee had to abandon the defense of Richmond and Petersburg.

April 2: In the morning, Lee was almost captured by advancing Federal soldiers, a telltale sign of Southern disintegration. As he started to evacuate Petersburg, he advised the government to leave Richmond. President Davis, who never thought that he would have to leave Richmond as long as Lee was defending it and who therefore ignored all distress signals, telegraphed back that he needed time to pack and to organize such an exit. For once, Lee lost his temper. He tore the message up and said sarcastically, "I am sure I gave him sufficient notice."

Federal artillery went into action. That night, Lee stood at a bridge to watch until his last soldiers crossed the Appomattox River. He was leaving Petersburg, with its warehouses deliberately set on fire, to the foe. The sky was filled with flames, and the city shook with the thunder of cannons. The bridge they used and the ammunition dumps were also exploded. Meanwhile, in Richmond, the same thing was happening: Government officials and troops were leaving, as bridges and ammunition dumps exploded and sent flames high into the sky. Factories, arsenals, warehouses, mills, even homes were destroyed by the retreating Southerners.

April 3: Even though other units rejoined Lee's army, it was down to 30,000. Still, after months of having been stuck in the trenches, Lee, like his soldiers, felt good being on the road at last, out in the open again, and confident of reaching Johnston in the South. But, whether Lee realized it or not, this was an escape, not a strategic maneuver.

One problem was that Grant, with a more direct and shorter route, would be able to outrace the Confederates. Another was that many soldiers, too weak for long marches, had begun to straggle. Lee's immediate goal was Amelia Courthouse, where he could reconcentrate his forces and obtain a much-needed store of food and supplies. Once he got there, however, he found that the supply system had broken down again. Artillery supplies were there, to be sure, but no food at all, and he had 30,000 starved, exhausted men with him.

Richmond had, in the meantime, fallen into the hands of roving mobs of starving people, who broke into abandoned depots and fought each other for food. Soon Federal troops occupied the capital and restored a semblance of order.

April 4: The failure of back-up services forced Lee to stop a day while food was sought from the surrounding country-side.

April 5: The wagons returned empty. No food was available anywhere. Two Federal armies were converging on Lee, taking advantage of the day he lost waiting for something to eat. They blocked his escape route. He decided to head westward to Lynchburg rather than to North Carolina. A forced night march resulted in crowding, confusion, and panic. Exhausted mules and horses fell down and hundreds of wagons had to be destroyed, even as the enemy cavalry harassed the marchers and captured many other wagons. Men, too, simply dropped in their tracks. In Richmond, Lincoln toured the streets and conferred with officials in Davis's abandoned Confederate White House.

April 6: Battles at Saylor's Creek and at Farmville cost another 8,000 men. Once again Lee learned of the unexpected disaster only after it had happened. He was down to 15,000 men, and his control over events was fast shrinking.

April 7: The Confederate troops finally obtained some food, but were subject to more harassment by the Federal forces. Lee found out, after his forces had crossed a river, that the bridge had not been burned completely, as he had ordered. The Federals were able to put out the belatedly started fire and get across too. The chance to gain some time and distance on the enemy, the chance to recoup the day lost by the hunt for food at Amelia, had been forfeited. This new mishap was the occasion for another of those once rare explosions of Lee's temper.

The mood grew darker. Lee advised his son Rooney, who had returned to action, "Keep your command together, General. Don't let them think of surrender. I will get you out of this."

At five P.M. Grant sent an official note suggesting the surrender of the Army of Northern Virginia. Lee consulted Longstreet, who replied, "Not yet." Lee was in a dilemma. On the one hand, it was his duty to fight on as long as there was the slightest chance of an escape and as long as his President, however unrealistic he might have been, expected that of him. On the other hand, as long as he had an army in the field, he could negotiate relatively good terms.

In his reply, Lee disagreed with Grant's observation that the position of the Confederate army was hopeless, but agreed with Grant in wanting to avoid useless bloodshed. He therefore wanted to know what terms were being offered as a condition for the surrender of the army. In seeking to avoid unconditional surrender, he was looking for an honorable way out.

April 8: Grant responded that he wanted Lee's men and officers disarmed. He stood ready to meet Lee. Meanwhile, Lee's army, its skeletal men dropping from exhaustion all over the march route, seemed to be falling apart even without pressure from an attacking foe. Lee was told that some officers, confronting the hopelessness of the situation, offered to make peace overtures to the Yankees in order to spare Lee "the odium of making the first proposal." He ruled that out. He had always taken full responsibility for everything that had happened, no matter how bad. He still hoped to be able to get his army away. Yet, realizing that the

chances were slim, he wanted to meet Grant while surrender was still only a choice and not yet a necessity. If Grant demanded, as was his habit in the West, unconditional surrender, Lee would choose death.

Lee had his last war council, and the decision was to hinge on the ability of the Confederate soldiers to fight another battle. The army was down to 8,000, with seventy-five rounds of ammunition per man. At Appomattox Courthouse, another brief battle against 80,000 men showed that little could be done. Nor was there any food for man nor animal. "Then there is nothing left for me to do but to go and see General Grant, and I would rather die a thousand deaths."

April 9, Palm Sunday: Lee appeared in the morning in full uniform; everything on him and on his horse was polished and clean. He vetoed the suggestion that the army disband and the men return to their respective states, and become guerrilla packs operating in the woods. Such continued and unorthodox warfare, he contended, would only bring suffering to many parts of the South not now directly touched by the war. Having fought as well and as long as was possible, they had to accept defeat. The men had to go home, plant crops, and "proceed to build up our country on a new basis." He was sure that Grant would not insist on unconditional surrender but rather give "as good terms as this army has the right to demand."

Naturally, some men—such as the dashing cavalier Southern officer type—wanted to go down fighting in a suicidal blaze of glory. Even Lee had toyed with the idea of merely placing himself at the front line to bring his miseries

to an end. He was, however, a moral being, a Christian, a conscientious Southerner, a man with a strong sense of responsibility for his soldiers and his fellow Southerners. He would not take that route, and he tried to deter others.

Perhaps nothing about Lee—not his military genius nor his personal nobility—was as great or as important as his decision on that day to seek reconciliation and a new beginning for the United States. With his unique military and moral prestige, he made it easy for others to follow suit. His argument was unanswerable: "It is our duty to live on. What will become of the women and children of the South if we are not here to protect them?"

Grant did not show up for the meeting, until Lee had sent three separate notes. The last one said what he had avoided saying and what Grant wanted him to say: "to discuss the terms of the surrender of this army." Finally, a meeting was set up in the McLean home in the village of Appomattox.

Lee arrived first and waited in the parlor. Then a bearded, slightly stooped man of average height entered wearing a soiled soldier's coat. It was General Grant. Lee met him halfway. The two generals of the opposing armies, long intent on destroying each other, shook hands and exchanged greetings: Lee the aristocratic, elderly man who had led a badly outfitted, outnumbered army in a glorious four-year campaign filled with victories that resulted in total defeat; Grant the young man with an unpromising background who belatedly took over the most modern military machine in the world, an army that went from one defeat to another until it achieved total victory by means of sheer numbers and the workings of time.

This was Grant's finest hour. As if inspired to rise to the

The McLean House, near Appomattox Courthouse, where Robert E. Lee surrendered, April 9, 1865.

level of events, as if aware that not only the world but also future generations would study his behavior here, Grant acted with kindness and deference. He did not force Lee to plead for anything, but conceded good terms beforehand. The two men began a new day in the relations between the North and the South. They were again fellow Americans consulting on a problem.

Grant began the meeting by recalling the one time he had met Lee, when both served in Mexico. After some more small talk, Lee raised the topic of the meeting and Grant proposed his terms: Officers and men were free to go home once they had been disarmed and all war supplies surrendered. Lee agreed. Grant wrote in pencil the draft of a memorandum to that effect and gave it to Lee to sign.

After correcting the accidental omission of a word, Lee thanked Grant for his having added that each soldier would be allowed to go home undisturbed. Then he had a favor to ask. He pointed out that in the Confederate Army, unlike in the Federal, the cavalry and artillery officers brought their own horses to combat. He wished therefore that they be allowed to keep the animals for farm work rather than be forced to hand them over as war materiel. Grant agreed to the suggested change. Lee indicated that this would be deeply appreciated by the Confederate men. Then Grant gave orders for Lee's men to be fed, and the formal documents of surrender were signed by the two commanders.

When the meeting ended, after about two or three hours, Lee rose, shook hands with Grant, bowed to all the Federal officers present and returned their salutes. On the porch, he looked into the far distance, and three times he hit his right fist into his left palm. As Lee mounted his horse, Grant and his officers came out of the house. The eyes of Lee and Grant met. Grant took off his hat, in a gesture of courtesy, and his officers followed suit. Lee did the same and, not saying a word, rode off to break the news to his soldiers.

On his return to his camp, his officers and men crowded around him, as they often had in better times. Lee told them, "Men, we have fought the war together, and I have done the best I could for you. You will all be paroled and go to your homes." Emotions cut off his words. He barely uttered, "Goodbye."

His men wept, or cursed, or rolled on the ground, or simply stood there, stunned, disbelieving. Finally, they were able to say goodbye to him. They pressed forward to touch him, or at least his horse, for one last time. They expressed their love for him, their undying faith in him. He rode on to his headquarters tent, and men along the way cheered him. And cried.

That evening, he oversaw the writing of his famous General Order Number 9. It begins: "After four years of arduous service, marked by unsurpassed courage and fortitude, the Army of Northern Virginia has been compelled to yield to overwhelming numbers and resources." Though Johnston still fought for a few more days in the South and though President Davis talked—incredibly—of yet winning, the dissolution of the only effective Confederate army ended the Civil War.

April 10: Demobilization of the Army of Northern Virginia began. Grant rode over to Lee's camp and had to wait. Learning at last of Grant's presence and annoyed by this rudeness on the part of his own men, Lee rushed over. They conferred briefly. Grant told Lee that if, as the most influential man in the South, he suggested surrender by all forces elsewhere, the bloodshed would finally end. Lee answered that when it came to Confederate forces other than his own, he would have to consult his President. Grant said he understood and dropped the point.

April 11: Demobilization proceeded all day.

April 12: The demobilization and paroling of the Confederate soldiers was at an end. His army disbanded, his job finished, Lee began his ride home, accompanied by a few officer friends. Everywhere along the way in Virginia news of his approach went before him. Women waited on the road with food for him. Children were brought out and held up so that they could tell their grandchildren of having seen the great man pass by.

April 15: He reached Richmond, at last. An especially large crowd was in the war-scarred streets awaiting him. Old people, children, women, wounded veterans surrounded him, greeted him, touched him, wept over him as had their sons, husbands, fathers, and brothers in uniform at Appomattox a few days before. At last, he reached home, entered, closed the door, and removed his sword for the last time. He dropped into his bed and closed his eyes.

Thirty-nine years as a soldier and four feverish years at the center of a hurricane were over.

12

Retirement, Recuperation, Reconciliation

(*April–September 1865*)

THE CATASTROPHE of defeat was quickly followed by another, entirely unexpected jolt. On April 14–15, at the very time that Lee was reentering Richmond and less than a week after the surrender at Appomattox, President Lincoln was assassinated. Southerners hated Lincoln, but wiser heads among them realized that this deed, no matter who was responsible for it, would do their cause no good. Lee expressed his shock and horror over the event. He urged the fleeing President Davis to make peace at once. The advice was, as usual, not followed.

For Lee, these must have been deeply depressing days. Yet if, being human, he sometimes glanced back at his own record of achievement in the Civil War, he had much to be proud of. He had fought ten historic battles, of which he had clearly won six; only one—Gettysburg—did he, perhaps,

Lee with his son, Custis, left, and an aide. This photograph was taken right after his return from Appomattox.

lose. In the two years in which he could operate freely in the field with a large force, he caused 145,000 enemy casualties at a cost of 103,000. Considering the vast disproportion in forces and equipment and considering that in every battle he was outnumbered by the enemy and therefore unable to follow up on the victory, this is a monumental feat. And these triumphs were achieved while Southern forces were being mismanaged and defeated nearly everywhere else in the Confederacy.

Though the war was over, Lee was still important to everyone. Grant saw the need to give Lee amnesty as a means of bringing about peace and reconciliation because most Southerners "will accept whatever he does as right, and will be guided to a great extent by his example." A central figure and a symbol, a monument in his own time representing all that was noble and heroic in the Old South and the lost cause, Lee was regarded as a leader, spiritually if not politically.

So it was that on May 5, 1865, General Meade visited Lee and urged him to take an oath of allegiance to the United States. Such an act—so different from Davis's refusal to give up—would inspire the South to follow his lead in making its peace with the North. Lee replied that he was a paroled prisoner of war and would do nothing until he knew how Washington proposed to treat the South. Meade said that the Federal government's policies would be determined by the Confederacy's giving signs of allegiance. Each side was waiting for the other to take the first step toward reconciliation.

At the other extreme, Lee faced the option of flight and emigration. Dyed-in-the-wool secessionists would never give in, never accept reunion with the North and emancipation of the blacks. They packed their bags and moved—or fled—to Canada, Mexico, Britain, or even Brazil. Some wrote Lee urging him to join them. His answer now, however, was what it had been in early 1861 to the Yankees: He would stay with his state, he would be loyal to Virginia, "and I prefer to struggle for its restoration and share its fate rather than give up all as lost."

That meant learning to live again with the victorious Northerners. No more now than during the war did he show any bitterness or vindictiveness toward the North. To people critical of the Yankees, he expressed the need for moderation. A good sign was that, as he noted, "General Grant has acted with magnanimity." Lee's policy in the postwar period was that "silence and patience on the part of the South was the true course." He himself, though called a traitor and rebel, never responded to the charges, never criticized anyone in turn. Controversies, he believed, only arouse emotions and obscure the truth.

After having been a leader of rebellious forces and a war hero, Lee became a man of reconciliation. He quarreled neither with his old enemy, the Northerners, nor with the Southern politicians who often shamefully let him down.

His continual advice to his veterans was, "Go home, all you boys who fought with me, and help build up the shattered fortunes of our old state." He himself did something like that. His last campaign—a moral rather than military campaign—was on behalf of peace and the revival of the South's prosperity in the face of the hostile exploitation by the conquering North.

Lee had earned the right to speak thus. This had been a

war he had warned against, disliked, would have prevented, predicted would last long—and done his best to win. Once the fight was over, however, further resistance was useless. He always believed in submission to legitimate authority, and now the force of arms had established, as it often does, whose authority was legitimate.

He wrote in 1865 that since the dispute between Virginia and the United States was settled by war rather than by persuasion and since the war was lost, wisdom required acceptance of reality. "The interests of the state are therefore the same as those of the United States." "True" patriotism and the desire to do right, he said, "sometimes requires of men to act exactly contrary at one period to that which it does at another." Hence it was that fighting for one's state against the United States had been honorable in 1861 and serving again the reunited nation was honorable in 1865.

On May 29, 1865, Lincoln's successor, President Andrew Johnson, offered amnesty, pardon, and full property rights to almost all Southerners who swore to support the Constitution and the laws of the United States. The only persons excluded were those who had been prominent in the Confederate ruling circles. They had to apply individually for amnesty in order to be judged case by case. This was the statement Lee had been waiting for before deciding to take an oath of allegiance. But there was no uniform policy in the land and soon afterward, a judge called a Federal grand jury to consider indicting Lee, with other Confederate leaders, on charges of treason. This development prompted a Unionist Senator from Maryland to offer himself as Lee's defense attorney: "In saving him I would be saving the honor of my country."

Lee decided that, if put on trial, rather than ask for pardon, he would face the charges and accept the outcome, whatever it might be. But had not Grant already given him and his army a pardon in return for surrender? Lee therefore wrote on June 13 to President Johnson a formal request to have all his rights restored. Letters of this type are usually filled with lengthy explanations and self-justifications; Lee's was brief. He was content to let his life and reputation speak for him. He listed only four items: graduation from West Point in 1829, resignation from the United States Army in 1861, appointment as general in the Confederate Army, and inclusion "in the surrender of the Army of Northern Virginia, April 9, 1865."

He sent this letter to Grant with an accompanying request that he endorse it. Grant immediately did so, adding an "earnest recommendation" that amnesty and pardon be given Lee. This letter to the President was the most controversial act of his life, and arguments over it in the South long outlived him. When Lee's action became known, many Southerners felt that they could follow their hero into acceptance of the Presidential amnesty. Others refused to do so, holding that the request for pardon was admission of a fault. Yet Lee was far more interested in moving on to new tasks than in raking over the past in order to find who was to blame. As it turned out, neither the indictment for treason nor the presidential pardon for Lee was carried through.

There were other threats and harassments. In late 1865, the radical Republican faction in the United States Congress, the postwar version of the prewar Abolitionists, succeeded in pushing for a severe policy toward the South. They wanted to exclude from the national legislatures any former officials of the Confederacy. As the man "at the head of the rebellion," Lee was called down to testify in Washington in February 1866. Nothing came of his remarks under close questioning.

Privately, Lee indicated that the radicals, knowingly or not, were doing their best to retain "bad blood" between North and South and to poison relations between blacks and whites. While the right to secede was now obviously ruled out and the abolition of slavery should be written into the Constitution, he still believed in strong states' rights. Specifically he found "obnoxious" the policy of the Federal government, under prodding from the radicals, to make the giving of the vote to blacks a condition of a state's readmission to the Union. To combat this policy he urged the election "of the most conservative eligible candidates." Lee might have been a moderate or a liberal compared to most Southerners, but next to many Northerners he was still a conservative man.

SOON AFTER starting a much-needed rest in his home in Richmond, Lee wanted to leave the noisy, bustling state capital and live "in some little quaint house in the woods." A wealthy widow gave him a home and some land on a large estate of hers. He and most of his family— his wife, his oldest son Custis, and his three surviving daughters, Mary, Agnes, Mildred—moved there in late June 1865. Life became easy and quiet. Lee loved the countryside better than any city.

Still, having worked conscientiously and hard all his life, he felt a certain emptiness in mere leisure. He wanted to find something to occupy his time. One possibility was public service. Not a few generals had entered politics. And indeed in 1867 people talked of having Lee nominated for the governorship of Virginia. Southerners would have turned out in droves to vote for this revered man, whose own father had become governor of Virginia after exemplary military service in the Revolutionary War.

But Lee hated politics, and his experience with the Confederate politicians during the war could only have soured him the more on it. The postwar political scene was in any case filled with noisy disputes of which he wanted no part. Any candidacy by him would, he feared, give the radicals the excuse to "excite hostility" to Virginia and its people.

There were other things to do—and offers to turn down. Many attempts were made to cash in on his fame, and he received various tempting proposals. A New York company offered him a job as president of the firm for $50,000 a year (a huge sum then); another offered a $25,000 a year job, and a third dangled $10,000 before him just for the use of his name. He indicated that his name was "not for sale at any price." An admiring nobleman overseas offered him an estate in England to live on in comfort, but again he turned it down saying: "I must share the fate of my people."

What he really wanted was honest money made from useful work. And, as a man now without a profession and with little money, he thought for a while of turning to farming, an occupation he had pursued at Arlington during the years 1857–1859.

Something else was nagging at him. He thought it important to give an accurate account of the war. He especially was eager for the world to know how outnumbered his army had always been. Urging his generals to write their memoirs, he planned his own history of his campaigns as a "tribute" and memorial to the Confederate men. Since many of the documents had been either burned or confiscated, he circulated a letter to his officers requesting documentation, especially for the last year of the war.

The assembly of material took longer than expected. He realized that it would take time for the truth to be known. Yet he kept at it, driven by the compulsion, the moral obligation, to advertise "what my poor boys, with their small numbers and scant resources, succeeded in doing." People little understood "the odds against which we fought."

Though he tried during the rest of his life to write his memoirs, he was never able to do it. The reasons were many. For one thing, he was not a practiced writer. And just as he had preferred to urge rather than order his generals, so now he did not like to be critical and judgmental of others. Perhaps, most important, he could not bear to go over all those experiences again. He almost never, in conversation or correspondence, touched on the war. Unlike Napoleon, who relived and refought and reinterpreted all his campaigns during his exile, Lee avoided talk of battles, personalities, controversies. "I do not wish to awaken memories of the past."

This does not mean that he regretted the past. On the contrary, when someone once spoke of "time lost" in the army, Lee vehemently replied that the time spent in the Confederate army was the "most profitably spent portion" of one's life, no matter what one went on to achieve later.

Or perhaps he did not write his memoirs because a new career suddenly opened up to him and took up a lot of his time.

13

College President
and Last Days

(1865–1870)

IN AUGUST 1865, Lee received his last major assignment, again one on behalf of his dear Virginia and the South. The trustees of Washington College in Lexington, Virginia, near the famous Virginia Military Institute, had elected Lee president of the school.

Here at last was an offer and a career that was attractive. Here was a task he was qualified for: to help the South by educating its younger generation. It gave him a dignified means of making a living, even as it satisfied his need to be of service to his state and country. He thought it important to teach the young "submission to authority" by his example. He also had a great belief in the value of education in bringing about a revival of the South and an elevation of its standard of living. The education of "all classes," including blacks, would promote Southern prosperity. He told a

Northern philanthropist that the best way to do something to benefit the South was to give money to a teachers' college.

His response to the trustees therefore was that though he no longer had the strength to teach class, he could undertake "the general administration and supervision of the institution." Typically, rather than ask, as most people would, if the school was prominent enough for someone like himself—it definitely was not!—he only asked if *he* had the academic credentials for the job. And with his usual concern for others, he worried that, since some people still considered him a notorious person, in accepting the job he might harm the college.

The trustees did not share his anxiety over his qualifications and his notoriety, and he was hired. Thanks to this employment, Lee's last years were happy, productive ones.

The school had been founded in 1749 and, when given a grant by George Washington, was renamed in his honor. (It is now known, naturally, as Washington and Lee University.) It had become a college in 1813, but during the Civil War it virtually ceased to exist. Lee was therefore not stepping into a job being vacated by someone else, but facing the challenge of bringing a dead school back to life. This is not exactly the sort of work a general is used to, but he had once been the Superintendent of no less a school than the West Point Academy for three years.

The half year's rest and recuperation from war was over. He was ready to begin normal life as a civilian after four decades in the army and to begin a new career at age fifty-eight in a strange town.

No mere figurehead president, he worked hard at his job and made a deep impression on the students and faculty

Lee in his office at Washington College.

there. Having little clerical help, the great, good, and famous General Lee attended even to menial tasks, sometimes over the protest of faculty and trustees. Yet there was time left over in the afternoon for one of his favorite activities— solitary rides into the nearby mountains on his horse Traveller. That animal had been with him through most of the battles. It was like a member of his family; horse and man loved each other. He also found time to garden, plant, repair stables, build walks.

Lee did an excellent job of reviving the school by increasing enrollment, upgrading the curriculum, molding the character of the students, bringing in money, and building up the campus. He began with four professors and fifty students, and within the year could count fourteen faculty members and 146 students. By 1867–1868, enrollment was up to 400 (and two dozen professors), with many students coming from out of state, some even from the North.

While he believed in the value of the classics and the pure sciences, he wanted departments that offered new areas of study, especially in the applied sciences, that is, modern technology. His emphasis on practical education made Washington College a trend setter. In five years he turned a nearly dead old-fashioned school into an admired pioneer in Southern higher education.

As might be expected, he was "permissive" in his administration. He pushed for a system of elective rather than required courses. Student behavior was governed by an honor system rather than the then-common elaborate rules, spying, adult supervision, and compulsory chapel attendance. He treated the students as he had his generals during the war, giving them full responsibility to work out for themselves the details of a plan—then for a battle, now for daily conduct at college. He insisted, however, on hard work from them, especially as their parents were making financial sacrifices in the postwar South to send them to college.

His presence was deeply felt at the college. He knew each student by name. Through fostering love and respect rather than fear, he exercised the greatest kind of authority. And in the main, because the students loved him, they behaved themselves.

Fund raising was a less attractive aspect of his job, especially as it sometimes required his presence in Richmond. Because of his name, though, he was successful at it. In 1867, the school was so prosperous that it could begin putting up new buildings, including an appropriate home for its president. His salary was increased. At his death, he was worth $88,000, a decent sum in those days—perhaps equivalent to a million or a half-million today.

Money for the school came from all parts of the country; eventually even Northern millionaires sent large sums. Yet sometimes, when money raising was done in the North by others on his behalf, it aroused anti-rebel sentiments and reopened old wounds. Some in the North (as Lee feared would happen when he originally joined the school) called Washington College a "treasonable institution" and declared Lee "not fitted to be a teacher of young men."

These were isolated outbursts. The trend was in the other direction. Even in his own lifetime, Lee was becoming an American hero, not just a Southern one. In fact, in the summer of 1868, there were suggestions that he be made the Democratic nominee for the presidency of the United States. Since Grant was to head the Republican ticket, it would have been a curious and exciting rematch of the old antagonists, this time in politics rather than battle. The *New York Herald*, in proposing him, expressed a view of him probably more widely held than were the attacks:

> Here the inequality will be in favor of the Democrats, for this soldier, with a handful of men whom he molded into an army, baffled our greater Northern armies for four years, and when opposed by Grant was only worn down by that solid strategy of stupidity that accomplishes its object by mere weight.

But the return engagement of champions was not to be. This, too, Lee refused.

In November 1868, Lee gave evidence before a grand jury looking into the charges of treason that the Federal government brought against President Davis. On the following day, he joined a party on a rail trip to Petersburg celebrating the remarriage of his son Rooncy. This was the railroad line he had defended for almost a year with his army. On the train ride, painful wartime memories came crowding back. He sat there depressed amid all the festivities.

But then something special happened. From the moment the train entered the city, crowds of cheering, worshipful people followed him. This visit marked a change in his life and outlook. For three years, grieving over the defeated, suffering South, he had buried himself in Lexington and in his work at the college. Now that he saw signs of reviving prosperity and joy, his spirits were raised, and he was more willing to travel, to meet people, to be less of a recluse.

Perhaps this new feeling was helped along by the dropping, in February 1869, of all indictments against him and his sons (and other military officers) for treason. The legal process had long since ceased being a serious threat, and it did not outwardly affect his life in any way. But to a man of Lee's sensitivity, it must have been painful to be considered a traitor in his own country. To know that he was officially at long last no longer a paroled prisoner of war must have meant a lot to his spirit. On a trip to Baltimore in May 1869, he paid a brief courtesy call on the new President, Grant, at the suggestion of the White House. It was another symbolic display of reconciliation and fraternization.

Still, Lee was not fully redeemed. The Fourteenth

Amendment to the Constitution effectively barred him from holding any state or Federal office. No less insulting to him was the permanent confiscation of relics of George Washington, from his Arlington home. These relics, he felt, rightfully belonged to his wife, the great-granddaughter of Martha Washington. Nor, despite legal maneuvers, was he ever able to get back the Arlington home itself. That had been the birthplace of his wife and children. That had been the property he had for two years worked to turn into a prosperous farm. He would not be able to pass on to his daughters the family inheritance.

By June 1869, his health was becoming a problem. He was suffering, according to contemporary diagnoses, from pericarditis or "inflammation of the heart-sac," from rheumatism of the back and arms, and probably from angina pectoris and arteriosclerosis. He had had a first flare-up of some of these ailments in 1863 during the campaign near Fredericksburg, and one other time during the war he was confined to bed for a while. In the summer of 1867 he was ill again. In October 1869, he became worse. He could walk only a short distance and suffered pain and difficulty in breathing. He talked of retiring to a little farm.

In March 1870, he gave up the presidency of the college and undertook a trip to the Deep South. He visited cities that he had known before the war or that had figured prominently in wartime battles—Savannah, Charleston, Columbia, Wilmington. It must have been a deeply satisfying and emotional journey. Everywhere he was given elegant dinners and greeted with huge cheering crowds. He met old friends, relatives, and officers. He met many of his former generals, who were now prospering in business, politics, or

Robert E. Lee in 1870 shortly before his death.

the professions. He visited the estate where the father he never knew well was buried. He visited the early home of his mother and the grave of one of his daughters. It was as if he were taking formal leave of the world by going back to his roots, by saying goodbye forever to friends and relatives, living or dead, and to places that were part of his past.

He was sixty-three but looked like an old man, hair all white, movement slow, posture stooped. In September 1870, while busy with local church affairs, he suffered a stroke. After lingering for two weeks, he died quietly on October 12. In his delirium he was haunted by the Battle of Gettysburg, as he said, "Tell [General] Hill he must come up."

His last words were, "Strike the tent."

The funeral of Robert E. Lee at Washington College, now Washington and Lee University.

SO ENDED the life of one of the greatest of all military figures.

Military geniuses are often sadistic, or ambitious, or money hungry, or self-centered, or self-righteous, or dictatorial. And if they did not have one or more of these vices to begin with, they get them as soon as success goes to their heads. Gentle people, on the other hand, are often ineffective in the world of deeds and achievements. It is hard to think of another human being who so ably combined the apparently opposite callings of being a general and being a true gentleman. It is hard to think of another person who was so gentlemanly a general or so militarily brilliant a gentleman.

No one else in history was quite like Robert Edward Lee.

FURTHER READING

I. On Lee

Davis, Burke. *Gray Fox: Robert E. Lee and the Civil War.* New York: Rinehart & Co., 1956.

Dowdey, Clifford. *Lee.* Boston: Little Brown & Co., 1965.

Freeman, Douglas Southall. *Lee,* 4 vols. New York: Scribner's, 1934–1935. Also available in a one-volume abridgment by Richard Harwell (1961).

Horn, Stanley F. *The Robert E. Lee Reader.* New York: Bobbs-Merrill, 1949.

Miers, Earl Schenck. *Robert E. Lee.* New York: Alfred A. Knopf, 1956.

II. On the Civil War

Catton, Bruce. *This Hallowed Ground.* Garden City: Doubleday, 1956.

Commager, H.S., ed. *The Blue and the Gray.* 2 vols. Indianapolis: Bobbs-Merrill, 1950.

Davis, Paxton. *Three Days.* New York: Atheneum, 1980.

Freeman, Douglas Southall. *Lee's Lieutenants.* 3 vols. New York: Scribner's, 1944–1945.

Hesseltine, W.B. *The Tragic Conflict.* New York: Braziller, 1962.

Nevins, Allen. *Ordeal of the Union.* 8 vols. New York: Scribner's, 1947–1971.

INDEX

PHOTO CREDITS